Y0-CXG-517

SPEAKING OF MAN

SPEAKING OF
MAN

BY

ABRAHAM MYERSON, M.D.

New York :: Alfred A. Knopf
1952

THIS IS A BORZOI BOOK,
PUBLISHED BY ALFRED A. KNOPF, INC.

*Copyright 1950 by Alfred A. Knopf, Inc. All rights reserved.
No part of this book may be reproduced in any form without
permission in writing from the publisher, except by a reviewer
who may quote brief passages in a review to be printed in a
magazine or newspaper. Manufactured in the United States of
America. Published simultaneously in Canada by McClelland &
Stewart Limited.*

PUBLISHED NOVEMBER 10, 1950
FIRST, SECOND, AND THIRD PRINTINGS BEFORE PUBLICATION
FOURTH PRINTING, FEBRUARY 1952

To ME man is a thickened node in the web of a universe of forces which, ever repetitively and ever anew, flow in and out of him; he is part of an ecology that involves plants, animals, climate, soil, and all kinds of radiant forces and chemicals. He is united by the invisible strands of heredity to every form of life that ever lived; and his fundamental drives and compulsive activities go back to the first piece of life that ever appeared on earth. He is packed with chemical factories, his every cell a better chemist and physicist than all the Nobel prize laureates put together. He is immersed in age-old and ever changing social forces that compress, enhance, destroy, or deform his trends. At every step he is beset by conflict between his biology and his sociology. He is the victim and the profiteer of his cunning hands and his fatal words. Within him there rages an inner turmoil made up of memories and especially words, the most important of which are "I," "you," "we," "they," and the most fatal, "you," when the man learns to address himself by this ominous term. Somehow there is a constant and shifting balance of forces in which hormones, ferments, enzymes, memories, ideas, emotions, and moods all play a part; and all of this is an unexplainable transit from conception to that catalytic dispersal, perhaps reassemblage, called death.

CONTENTS

SPEAKING OF MAN

PRELUDE:

ON THE WORTH OF LIVING

RECENTLY the Angel of Death fluttered around me, and it seemed for a while that he would win the battle from my devoted doctors. For the time being, however, he has abandoned the attack, although he has left me ripe for the plucking and my possible life span is a short one.

During my illness and since, in my semi-invalidism, I have read very intensely and extensively, especially those books which deal with God, Man, and the Universe; in brief, religion, philosophy, and science. Long ago, when I was young and before I became engrossed in a professional career, I read ardently of theology, philosophy, the history of man, and the history of his beliefs. I gave up religion and philosophy quite completely during the years of my young manhood, maturity, and middle life. Occasionally I read Plato as a soporific. But when the bed became my chief abode, as it did in September 1947, I thought I would go back to the reading of my youth and see whether my skepticism and rejection of absolutes of any and all kinds could change, now that old age and sickness had descended upon me. I did not crave consolation; I felt no fear that needed assuagement; and I had no yearning for immortality that demanded faith in God and a future life. I read, and I read, and I read — religion and the history of religion, philosophy and the lives of the philosophers, the new and the great of recent science, and the scientists who try to reconcile religion and science. I came out of this debauch of reading as unregenerate as I went in. The Angel of Death is no angel to me; he is not a *he* at all, but a part of the cycle of life and death; and I understand quite well how, sooner or later, I am to disappear as an entity and re-enter the cycle, in fragments that do not include consciousness and a soul. The *why* of life and death completely eludes me and, I believe, eludes even those who proclaim their transcendent ability to know it.

I hope to have the time to set down in unhurried fashion certain attitudes toward life and living which my experience, including my reading, has consolidated within me. I shall not cite authorities, nor the chapter, verse, and page of books, for I have done too much of that in my scientific writing. Here I beg leave to indulge myself in a more scattered, more reflective, less rigorous discussion of the problems that beset me in my work and that beset the reader in his life. My illness has sharpened my appetite to do this that I have long wished to do; more importantly, it has paradoxically given me the "time" that I needed. I believe my mind to be as keen as ever it was, and I am going to hew to the line, perhaps for the first time in my life.

I ask myself: Why do I write at this time when my energy barely suffices for mere living? I know the answer, which has reasons to bolster it and yet may not be reasonable. Perhaps I am expressing a stubborn pride in myself, an unwillingness to concede defeat, a bravado in the face of death. I know that man's foreknowledge of his own death is responsible for the growth of the other-worldliness of religion and is behind most of the scurrying activities of this fear-ridden planet, from its most predatory self-seeking to the vastest and most ambitious world plans. "Eat, drink, and be merry, for tomorrow we die," is one way man has faced his demise; "live so that each day you are more fit for heaven" is its reverse. Whatever may lurk in my unconscious about my last efforts on the earth's surface, this book symbolizes a theory of worth-while living, which I here present, believing that it is good. I am a skeptic in many of my "beliefs," but not in my ways of life. I believe that, willy-nilly, man will continue to live on this earth; that somehow I am bound to my fellows so that I wish them well and must work for and with them. I feel in myself so strong a sense of continuity with life that I want to leave behind my self within the covers of a book. Whether I shall make myself felt — that I know nothing about.

There are three dimensions to worthwhileness of life or living. One is duration, which has no value in itself, but gives the framework of value to everything else. A long life is no unqualified blessing. I have seen very miserable people to whom each day was a torture, who outlived family, friends, and physicians, and I have seen utter futility prolonged long after the end had come to the mind itself.

The second dimension is the interest, satisfaction, and happiness that the man himself experiences. To live for others is an aim few can have unless their own desires and satisfactions are sufficiently reached. Egoism has its place in the sun, and while some are capable of spurts of unalloyed altruism, this basic second dimension anchors a man to prosaic reality.

The third dimension is usefulness to others. I believe that there is an instinctive basis to altruism, that not everything one wants is selfishness, even though the unselfishness may be part of selfhood. One must differentiate between the selfhood of a gangster and that of a philanthropist, between the hate of the self-seeker and the love of the self-sacrificer. I avoid the term "doing good," although I tend to despise those who use the term "do-gooder" as a reproach. I avoid it merely because being useful implies a more direct fulfillment of the altruistic spirit.

There may be a fourth dimension to the worthwhileness of life which, paradoxically, denies it except as a preparation for a next world. It will be sufficiently clear that I reject this fourth dimension for myself, but I have no quarrel with those who accept it, provided they do not persecute the unbeliever.

Be that as it may, to those who accept at least my three dimensions of life, I extend my comradely greeting.

Chapter I

MY FATHER AND I DISCUSS MATTERS

This was my father's favorite story:

A conclave of scholars once discovered that no one had ever defined what a scholar — the word and the man — really was; so they set about making a definition. One man said this and another said that, and there was a very lively scholastic debate until an elder rose to finish the discussion.

"A scholar," he said, "is like a pin, which must, as you know, have a good sharp end, as well as a good round end. The scholar's sharp end is to think with, his round end is to sit down to the job with. If he has only the sharp end he becomes a dilettante flitting from job to job, accomplishing little. If he has only the round end, he is a pedant, unimaginative and uninspired. Yes, the scholar must have a good sharp end and a good round end."

This old scholar might have stated that the good round end and the good sharp end are the two essentials of good living. The round end symbolizes endurance, the animal capacity to take it; the sharp end the human ability to learn by experience. Thus, combining animal endurance and human intelligence, one might at last hope to thread one's way through the maze of life.

My father and I, living in worlds apart so far as daily activity was concerned, he a former teacher and then a small businessman, and I an active teacher, research worker, and psychiatrist, were unified by a common goal in our thinking and seeking. Whenever we met, we discussed two subjects that have engrossed scholars from the beginning of thinking: first, the nature of wisdom, and secondly, the nature of man. What is wisdom, and who is the wise man? We found no definitions that held together against analysis and criticism. We made provisional delimitations and established, to our own satisfaction, some general functions of the wise man and of wisdom.

The wise man continues to hope, but not to expect much of life or of man. This is the beginning of wisdom. He governs his passions and desires, but does not crucify them, because he reflects that there may be and probably is a wisdom of instinct that precedes and defies the wisdom of reason. As he reviews the history of the human mind, he sees no reason, paradoxically, to deify Reason.

The wise man is not an ascetic. His is not a bloodless life, a burned-out wisdom. Therefore it is wrong to picture the truly wise man as old. The only positive wisdom is attained while the individual is young. There must be struggle within for balance, strength, and harmony. Wisdom is not, therefore, obtained when instincts and passions retreat into nonexistence. The wisdom of nondesire, wherever found, is the wisdom of retreat. Between the overstriving, let us say, of the American life and the nirvana of Buddhism, there is that medial place in which the wise man lives.

The wise man does not expect, although he hopes for, intellectual or moral greatness in the high places of the world of power; there he expects the qualities by which men achieve, and especially keep, power; namely, cruelty, cunning, and an eloquence that in reality is usually a gift for the distortion of fact and a tool for the inflaming of passions. In places of power the wise man expects to find people who are willing to kill, and sometimes even to be killed, to achieve their purposes, thus gaining advantage over the softer, more humane, less hardy people of the world. But he never loses the hope that some day power and intelligent philanthropy will come together in great men.

The wise man does not expect consistency or harmony in the pattern of his own life or any other man's life, for he sees that man is a mosaic of characteristics and qualities that only rarely achieve an internal and intrinsic harmony. He notes that the individual is a collection and accidental juxtaposition of discordance and agreement. Although men may achieve some degree of harmony through struggle and through the pressure of life, that harmony, alas, is as often achieved through the destruction of qualities as through their blending, as in the case of the ascetic or the man of power.

The wise man sees the grim contradiction between the built-up intelligence of man, as expressed in tools, mechanical and scientific creativeness; and his incapacity and inability to use these tools humanely and kindly. He knows that the competing group life of nations is as feral and savage as ever, yet he sees, as the basis of his hope for the future, that private life has become more sane, more reasonable and less cruel than it was.

The wise man knows that courage and a love of truth make some men defy the opinions of the crowd. He himself is not too courageous. Like Montaigne, he often waits until the active span of his life is over and then he writes the truth as he dares express it. There is undoubtedly some cowardice in all wisdom, and some folly in all courage.

My father and I finally agreed that the wise man has to know his fellow man and life far more than he needs to know books. Scholarship is only a means and not an end. The man who retreats to scholarship as an end retreats from wisdom and from life. The beginning and end of wisdom, therefore, is search and research into the nature and organization of man.

All this was preliminary to the main question of our mutual discussion. We asked ourselves: What is man?

The zoologist defines man as *Homo sapiens*. This he clearly is in his potentialities, for he has the capacities to reason, to think, and to act reasonably and thoughtfully. But knowledge or, better, reason is not the outstanding characteristic of his nature. It may serve to distinguish him from the animals of other types, just as the robin redbreast may be distinguished from some sober-hued bird by its bright color. But distinction is not definition, and the reason of man, we believed, is a quality too sparsely used to distinguish Homo. At the best, human reason dominates only a few spheres of his activity.

It seemed to us just as appropriate to call man *Homo rationalis*, because we see continually, in both his personal and his communal history, that he uses his reason to justify his prejudices, to find more scope and more techniques for his passions and biases, to give reasonable-ness to his unreason. This is said to be wishful thinking, and true it is that man thinks mainly in the interest of his desires and wishes. But I have seen men in melancholic mood think against their interests of survival and in the interest of self-destruction. Thus rationalization may bet-ter be called the "modalization" of thinking; that is, man thinks according to the nature and intensity of his moods.

Homo sensualis is another name for *Homo sapiens* in the light of his actual history. His sensual drives include all the pleasures and voluptuousness of his body. From the instinctive drives and pleasures of the body he builds up conscious desire, refinement, epicureanism, connois-seurship, and often perversion. He lives more directly and purposefully for the pleasure of his body than any other animal, using his great powers of tool-making and of speech for this purpose. He creates artificial foods and even builds up new chemicals with which to intoxicate his organism. His sexual life is incomparably more sen-sual than that of any other animal; perhaps the fact that the mates face each other in the sexual embrace and thus participate in a mutual intimacy more complete than that of any other creature accounts in part for this. He has exercised his ingenuity and resourcefulness in a conscious manner to build up all kinds of sensual and sexual ac-tivity. For most creatures in the world, the motivating drives are fundamentally unconscious and instinctive, but man consciously evolves and distorts his tastes and satisfactions. Instinct has thus become shot through with self-consciousness and intelligence, often to its perversion and destruction.

Side by side with this sensual trend, we found that

Homo sensualis is also *Homo asceticus*, despising his body, hating it, declaring large segments of its activities obscene, attempting to crush and interdict its urges, declaring of his own reproduction that it is fundamentally vile and can be sanctified only by curious procedures. This hatred of the body, of pleasure, of satisfaction, is peculiarly human; there is nothing else in the universe to compare with it.

We turned then with horror to human history and the human scene and saw that we might call man *Homo ferociens*. Except for that curious antagonist and protagonist of man, the insect, there is no other creature that masses itself in great multitudes and sets out to destroy other multitudes of its own species. The cruelty of animals is, on the whole, incidental to their life purposes. The cruelty of man expresses itself in a thousand and one directions, independently of any need, and often as an instrument of that grim intoxicant, power.

But here again, side by side with this, man demonstrates the opposite trend. He shows more tenderness than any other living animal and feels a more conscious love than is found elsewhere in the universe. There has been a gradual penetration of the social structure by tenderness, which my father and I traced from the home, where it started as the love of the mother (and in a lesser degree of the father) for the child, and then infiltrated to some extent into society. The home at least was the one place where tenderness gradually became the dominant and expected attitude. There is no original tenderness in the primitive expression of sexuality, because sex is an appetite and not a sentiment. A civilizing alchemy has fused this appetite with tenderness; and the fusion is an ideal relationship, even though it is often artificial and often breaks. From time to time, as we surveyed history, we saw that men arose who expressed by their lives and by their words the most complete tenderness and were, in fact, its human embodiment. The ascendancy of tenderness in many of the human relationships offers one of the hopeful signs on the arena of man's life.

Here we came to an underlying and fundamental principle in human life, its ambivalence. It seemed to us proper to call man *Homo ambivalens*, a creature who builds up contradictory, hostile, and opposite patterns of life and attempts to live them simultaneously. He swings from one extreme to another, extolling sensuality, crucifying it, enhancing and amplifying the role of instinct, and at the same time denying and depriving instinct of its chance for biological and legitimate expression. We saw this ambivalent attitude toward himself and his purposes as a general operating principle everywhere in human life. In a sense, then, man is schizophrenic and has built up deep contradictions, which tax his strength and his sanity.

And so we looked and found *Homo tool-maker* and *Homo word-maker*, tools and words being the final expression of the magical wish-goals of man, his will to conquer and his longing to fulfill his heart's desire by a wand and a magic concatenation of words. The tools he has built involve man in one of the sharpest contradictions of his nature: to wit, as a tool-maker he is *Homo sapiens* to the highest degree, and as a tool-user he is either *Homo ferociens* or something quite crude and stupid.

The geniuses of the race have built tools that surpass the magical accomplishments of fairy tales; the vulgar and cruel of the world have taken over and controlled these tools.

The words fashioned by man's cunning brain and facile tongue have also served him in contradictory fashion. They have enabled him to build up a conscious racial continuity, so that the most ancient and the most remote writer and speaker can still command an audience. The Word transmits the noblest thoughts and the most magnificent accomplishments of man; the Word carries on social heredity as the seed transmits biological heredity, but, like the latter, it carries with it social diseases as well as social advancement.

My father and I traced these and many other curious matters back to that hatred of loneliness and that fear of self which make man *Homo gregariens*. Little groups, big groups, the couple, and the mob — there is in these, in the last analysis, no individual Homo, however oppressed by self-consciousness a man may become. Even in the deepest solitude a hermit does not escape his fellows, because the words and the ideas by which he peoples his staked-out world have been fashioned by others. Gregariousness is the real human fact; it gives all the potency of praise and blame, reward and punishment, exhilaration and shame. It bestows all the power and the meaning of leadership and followership, of command and obedience; it crushes the defeated and lifts up the victorious. It cries out: "Believe, believe"; and man, the credulous, believing the fantastic and nonsensical, even glories in his ability to believe the unprovable and absurd. There is no limit to the herd passivity, no bottom and no top to the swinging and shifting ferocity and submission of the mass. A blind instinct holds men together. Reason may demur; intelligence may jeer; but something deeper and more powerful than these newcomers on the scene overwhelms them and makes them yield obeisance.

These and many other peculiarities of Homo did we discuss and ponder. At one time my father said: "You must crown your life's efforts by a book on man. Treat the subject as objectively as we have talked these many times, and yet let neither your indignation nor your wonderment slip out of your writing. For man cannot be dispassionate about man, nor should he be. Neither does it seem to me that a satirical account of the contradictions and follies of human behavior is now of any value. That kind of thing has already been done too much, and is a cheap exercise of the intellect, like doing handsprings to make fun of cripples. No, a book about man should have only enough satire to season its profound seriousness."

My father finally said: "Objectivity, yes; a dispassionate account of man and his deeds, yes; but only if in the final analysis one adds sympathy and understanding to the story. Without these tenderness disappears and there is nothing to life whatever, nothing to any book about life."

On October 17, 1938, in the eighty-eighth year of his life, my father died. His beloved wife, my mother, had passed along the year before, after having lived with him for sixty-six years of complete devotion. After her death he waited patiently and calmly for his own end, because the desire to live had now gone. On the day before his death I noticed that his lips were blue and told him that he must rest in bed to give his aged heart a chance to recuperate. He smiled and went to bed. The next morning I found him in a near-by park discussing with some elderly men the ways of the world and man. When I reproached him for his rashness, he asked me with a twinkle in his eyes: "How much life will you guarantee me, O doctor, if I obey your orders? And how much value shall I place on a month, six months, a year more of that chronic illness, extreme old age?" So I smiled at him and left him with his friends.

That night after a pleasant supper he suddenly turned to his housekeeper and asked her to lay out his nightclothes and to call his sons, for he felt very weak. He undressed himself, got into bed, and quickly lapsed into a coma, and thence to a death that was far more peaceful than any other I have witnessed. The body made no struggle; there was no harsh breathing, no death rattle. There was just the transition from activity to passivity without the disturbing and chaotic expression of the blind, bodily will to survive. He had died as philosophically as he had lived.

So he passed on, and therefore I turn to the writing of this book. I am what the world rightly calls an elderly man. Out of a full quiver of experience, out of an intimate collaborative thinking with my father, out of a deep desire that springs from sources I am not eager to discover, I write this book.

Chapter II

MY PREJUDICES AND PREPOSSESSIONS

*Björnson says that there was once a skeptic who
was finally killed by his colleagues. As
they stood musingly around his dead
body, one said: "There lies a man who
kicked the whole world around like a
football." The dead man opened one
eye. "Ah, yes," said he, "but I always
kicked it toward the goal."*

I⊤ is now ten years since my father died, and I have
only very recently turned to the writing of this book. The
war years came and went, leaving behind a world with
a shocked and shocking social climate. I do not wish to
draw a picture of the world as I see it, but certainly there
is neither peace nor peace of mind. Nor can I conceive
of any man having peace of mind with affairs as they are
unless he be stupid, callous, or intoxicated by some immediate and personal good fortune. Fortunately, or unfortunately, almost all of us live in a private world in
which the meaning and value of events are the greater
to us the nearer these are to its center — ourselves. We
raise our voices in lamentation if death or disaster hits
near to that center, but we can bear with considerable
philosophy the deaths by starvation of a million poor

devils in China. Yet the threat to each of us is now so great that the winds of anxiety are ever blowing in today's social climate.

Let me state certain of my prejudices and prepossessions so that no one will be misled into the reading of this book. Every serious writer dips his pen into the fluids of his own life, and each reader approaches a book so written with the hope of finding no assault on his deepest and guiding beliefs. It is thus only fair that without too much argument and certainly without proof I declare certain controversial attitudes of my own and thus free myself in advance from reproach.

At the very outset I shall say that I do not believe that so insignificant and puny a creature as man, living on a fragment of matter lost in the immensities of the universe, can know anything about absolutes, whether these are called God or another name. There is a group of men who know about God in detail, professionals who have arisen, so I think, to answer the age-old cry of man for certainty. They are priests, ministers, rabbis, and theologians of various cults and degrees of holiness. I have known some of them intimately and have never met one who seemed a reasonable object of inspiration from on high. Good fellows, yes; learned men, certainly; some mere professionals, others honest but very troubled within. Actually, none of them claims any direct personal knowledge of the absolute or good, but they all refer for authoritative proof to an ancient book, written with grandeur but filled with biological and historical error; or to St. So-and-so who, living in an era when credulity was very high and knowledge very scarce, knew much less about factual matters than a child of our own time.

I cannot swallow the stories of miracles, which are believed in direct proportion to the distance in time from our days, the general state of ignorance of the time of their occurrence, and the fierceness and intolerance of belief. I have rejected all existing authorities on the matter because the Bible, the Koran, revelations of the Latter-day Saints, and the opus by Mary Baker Eddy differ not in credibility but in style. The more absolute and orthodox a religion, the more intolerant are its devotees and the greater the schism between its doctrines and the scientific facts of life. To glorify faith, per se, is quite nonsensical to me. Faith in what? is the question I ask. I am sure the priests and followers of Moloch did not lack faith in bloody human sacrifice. The early followers of Mahomet fought with zeal because they knew that nothing was more real than the houris awaiting them in paradise. "I believe because it is absurd," which to theologians is so praiseworthy an affirmation, is an absurd statement of belief to me.

I see no reason to believe that those to whom revelation came in former days were different or more reliable than they are now. I know that when saints abounded, men believed with a directness and completeness rare today. Of course they also believed the world was flat, were sure that there were witches and wizards, and explained natural phenomena in a fantastic or supernatural way. Credulity reigned as an absolute monarch, and skepticism and heresy were the greatest of sins. Like men, ideas and beliefs may be judged by the company they keep, and even today the faithful of every religion are, with some exceptions, the least educated and the least able intellectually. Perhaps knowledge is bad, perhaps intelligence is a curse, perhaps the Sicilian peasant or the Lithuanian ghetto-dweller is nearer reality than the great university professor or the scientists who are conquering space, time, and matter. I shall continue to reject revelation and the evolved theology of professional religionists until it becomes normal and *not* schizophrenic to hear and see God and the angels. A double standard of morals is held to be reprehensible; a double standard of belief is even worse.

Besides the professionals, there is another group who also know God and the absolute. This group has had a great claim on my sympathy, and my principal activities in life have been to understand and help them. I mean, of course, the mentally sick, those who because of illness have such grave distortions as delusions and hallucinations. Go to any hospital for the mentally ill, and among one thousand patients you will find at least twenty-five who have received personal communication from the Deity or at least from a dead saint, or who have won for themselves the panoply of deity or sainthood and are the fortunate repositories of complete and absolute knowledge.

Just before an epileptic attack there takes place what is known as the aura. Occasionally this aura is the feeling that one is about to be told the secret of the universe and be initiated into the select group of those who know the All. Alas, the convulsion comes, the initiation does not take place, and the All remains the unknown.

Indeed, were a man to be brought before a jury of leaders of all the great churches and theologians of whatever kind you please, claiming that he heard and saw God, that he was directed in what he did by God's voice, that he had come to enunciate a new doctrine by which the world would achieve eternal salvation, I believe the jury would agree with psychiatrists and everybody else that he was insane and needed to be in a hospital. In other words, that which was holy in less critical times has become psychiatric in our day. Frankly, I see no reason to believe that holiness changes its nature just because it occurs in a different century.

Nor have I much in common with most of the philosophers, those curious folk of whom Whitehead said: "The besetting sin of philosophers is that being merely men, they endeavor to survey the Universe from the standpoint of God." They reach the absolute not as the pious do, by act of faith or some private revelation, but by syllogism and the reasoning process. But the reasoning process leads to so many and such confusing points of view that one can arrange philosophers and philosophies in a sort of spectrum in which each wave length claims to be the absolute in wisdom and logic. It seems to me that every basic philosophy, thoroughly and consistently developed, leads sooner or later to a world in which a man cannot and does not live. Let me cite just two philosophic solutions of consciousness and reality and see where they bring us and, more pertinently, how far they were reflected in the lives of their great proponents.

Consider the views of Bishop Berkeley — that since

all we know flows into us via the avenues or the alley-
ways of our consciousness, therefore there is no reality
besides or outside of our consciousness. It is true that the
first part of this idealistic philosophy has been accepted
by many who do not go on to the second part of the
thesis. One of the greatest objective scientists of all times,
Galileo, agreed that what we saw, smelled, tasted, and
felt was not reality, but only the way reality comes to us,
either through the senses or through those instruments
which we evolve to magnify, measure, and refine our
sensory experiences. Surely there are roads to realities of
which we know nothing, and our nervous system and its
appendages and attachments are pathetically limited,
compared with the possibilities of sensory knowledge.
For example, we have no direct electronic pathway from
the world to ourselves. Conceivably some creatures
might have such a sensory road, although what they
would be like we cannot really imagine; perhaps they
would resemble an X-ray plate more than a man. Even if
the world goes away when I lose consciousness, or if it
filters into me in the form of vague and evanescent
dreams when I sleep, to conclude that the world exists
only in my own head leads to the well-known *reductio
ad absurdum* of solipsism, a world created by each man
and peopled only by his consciousness. Bishop Berkeley,
of course, did not and could not live by this consistent
nonsense, which is really what all rigorous logic finally
becomes. He lived *as if* the people he met were real and
depended not at all upon him for their existence, even if
they did disappear when he closed off his senses, and reappeared when he opened them. To fall down a stairway

that you do not see hurts as much as to fall down one you
do. If you conclude consistently that the automobile
whose horn you hear is created by your auditory consciousness, you may not live to learn your mistake.

Let me turn to a great scientist, the founder of a line
of brilliant men, a biologist of the first water and a fighter
who pulled no punches. Thomas Henry Huxley, the
scientist, in his capacity as philosopher suffered from the
prepossession that he must be consistent. So Huxley reduced Consciousness, which Berkeley made the All in
All, to the Nothing at All, a mere hiss of the steam of the
engine of life. Bodily processes, brain processes, mind
processes — these went on in a chain of antecedents and
sequences, and Consciousness, by the light of which
Huxley wrote and worked, was — he said — an epiphe-
nomenon of no real significance. It therefore followed
that an unconscious Shakespeare could, as someone said,
have written his grand works; and the ups and downs
of this flame of the mind, this illumination of succes-
sive patches of the universe, need not have happened
at all.

Thus was launched a philosophic movement that
finally culminated with the statement of the behaviorists
that only conduct is important and all the introspection
in the world matters not at all since it cannot be measured
and weighed. The only reality the individual knows is
thus ruthlessly taken away; the inner life that seems to
give value to each event is a hideous jest on the part of
some One or some Thing. One can accept such a philosophy only for a purpose, to work out a hypothesis and
to avoid entanglement with the subtleties and difficulties

of introspection; but one cannot live by it. Our own lives, our continuities and our separations, our binding and blinding emotions, have no value or meaning except as we somehow consciously experience them. Thomas Henry Huxley's most intense moments of consciousness very likely were those in which he was proving by written argument, which he knew would come to the consciousness of others, that consciousness was of no importance whatever.

I am grateful for the day, years ago, when I discovered Hans Vaihinger and his philosophy of "as if," although Kant also talked of "as if" as a way of living. Nothing can really be known, so one must live by certain "as if's" — as if it were worth while, as if there were a continuity of purpose and achievement, as if it were better to be humane than cruel, as if love were an end in itself.

Another conclusion of Vaihinger's has meant more to me than almost any other intellectual concept of my life, and that is that in human life there is always the great danger that the means tend to predominate over the ends. In a dozen and one fields of science and social relationship, technique in general becomes more worshipped than what is sought. It thus comes about that how outweighs what, and that the manner of doing, from eating to procreation, is more important than the purpose of the act itself.

A man has a job to do; let us say that his purpose is to build a table. Thus he visualizes the construction of something upon which a dinner may be served or art objects may be placed. From the beginning of craftsmanship men have developed a technique for building this table. Let us call this technique the means that the carpenter is to use to fulfill his end. The carpenter accumulates wood of the proper stock, assembles a set of tools, and goes to work. The means are as simple as the final product warrants. The carpenter sings no ceremonial songs and dances no symbolic dances at the beginning, the middle, or the end of his job. The plane and the saw he uses are strictly utilitarian. He does not make them extraordinarily large, or give undue time to the use of any of the instruments. The means, in other words, in this highly utilitarian procedure, are strictly subordinated to the end. The end governs the selection of tools and the technique of using them.

One of the threats that the discerning eye sees at the bottom of much of the trouble as well as much of the beauty of human society is that the means tend to get out of control and become dominant over the end. The law, for example, has the object of dispensing justice by intervening in the disputes of men and, more importantly, laying down the rules and regulations within which they shall live with one another. There then develop courts of law, where the technique becomes so cumbersome and the procedure so intricate that decisions are finally based not on justice, but on the means used — that is, on *whether or not the procedure has been carried along from stage to stage with legality and propriety.* Every lawyer and every judge, as well as every observant layman, knows that legality has become a professional game; and the connoisseur in the law delights as much in the game, the means, as in the final end, justice, and perhaps more so.

The law itself has recognized this and attempts are being made to shorten trial procedure, to take certain cases out of the regular course of the courts, with their delays and their finickiness. It is curious to note, however, that while this may succeed for a time, it eventually fails because the same error is sooner or later repeated. Industrial accident boards are a case in point. They were established with the aim of achieving informal trials, but since lawyers are usually appointed as commissioners, and since lawyers appear for plaintiff and defendant, the result has become a formal trial with its emphasis on means, the technique of procedure. Also in the field of law is the contract, one of the great bases of human intercourse. Since it gives a stability to the relationships between men, it would seem essential to keep it simple so that both contracting parties might understand what they are doing. The reverse takes place. By a multiplication of words, clearness is lost and contracts are made so complicated that only a specialist can understand them.

Consider a great historical situation, the establishment of a new society based on communal ownership of the means of production and distribution. To bring this about, the establishing group has to develop a technique of power and use the weapons of guile, stratagem, and finally of bloodshed. Later, to maintain what they have achieved, they still have to use the same means, use *power* to keep power. The inevitable result is a new caste system rather than the communistic ideal. This is the tragedy of all human idealism, since each idealism must utilize the weapons of battle to establish itself.

What it finally wins is a successful war rather than a successful idealism.

If we view religion, the same is seen to be true. Whenever a great ethical and spiritual leader proclaims some simple, elevating doctrine, his followers must adorn the simple faith with complex ceremonials and techniques so as to capture the imagination of the common man and establish the doctrine successfully. The end thus shifts from the establishment of an ideal to the means of capturing and holding the allegiance of *Homo creduliens* and *gregariens*. Endless rituals are introduced. The minutiæ of worship become more important than the worship itself, and great wars have been waged over mere words of an incomprehensible nature. The difference between *homoiousion* and *homoousion*, for example, ostensibly caused bloody civil wars in the Holy Roman Empire and finally split the Christian world in two.

The most devastating application of this principle is to thought itself. Vaihinger says that while thought was originally only a means in the struggle for existence, we have gradually lost sight of its original practical purpose and now practice it for its own sake as theoretical thought. Through thought we try to solve such impossible problems as those of the origin and meaning of the universe. The origin of logic was the great technological development of thought. Then logic became an end in itself, as in the endless cogitations and speculations of the scholastics of the Middle Ages and of the Jewish rabbis and Christian churches. Somehow it is assumed that logic is a perfect instrument, whereas its very syllogistic beginning, the familiar "All men are mortal, Soc-

rates is a man, therefore Socrates is mortal," is only cir-
cular reasoning replete with fatal flaws. Some men become so absorbed in the fine instrumentation of thought,
in the delicate and beautiful words it can employ, in the
long chain of symbols and metaphors it can construct,
and in its actual practical accomplishments, that they
forget what thought is for and live not to do but merely
to think. The best that thought can do is to build up
practical schemes for making plastic and elastic the activities of the organism and create long-range programs
of activity, legitimately enough on a hypothetical basis,
but without involving itself in abstractions, which are its
imperfect creations. "It is because our conceptual world
is itself a *product* of the real world that it cannot be a
reflection of reality," states Vaihinger. The humbler
thought remains as a means, the more it achieves. The
more arrogantly it proclaims itself as an end, the greater
its catastrophes.

These are pertinent and revealing questions to ask oneself from time to time: Am I letting the means by which
I live dominate my life so that they have become more
important to me than all else? Have I become too
wrapped up in ceremony, form, refinement, and technique? Am I losing simplicity, vigor, and endurance?
Have I built up so dense a forest of means that all I can
see are leaves and branches and no trees? Are my purposes becoming obscured as I elaborate the ways and
means of doing and forget to do? To seek from time to
time a clarification of purpose and a simplification of
means becomes a prime need of the individual and of the
group.

Probably more pertinent than my philosophic declarations, since I am no philosopher, are my prejudices and prepossessions on psychiatry. Because I am perhaps a very prejudiced person and certainly a combative one, it is best to warn the reader that it is in just this light that most psychoanalysts regard me. Although I have all the respect in the world for the honest hypothesis, I am not easily convinced. "As if" has opened more magical doors than "abracadabra."

I believe that Freud was wrong in his theories of dreams, concept of complexes, emphasis on infantile sexuality, idea of the death wish, division of the personality; and I do not see that he has helped in any significant degree to cure mental disease. Although I may be wrong, I believe that he was a writer and philosopher and not primarily a scientist. While symbol and metaphor are the very essence of poetry, they are quite out of place in any science except mathematics. Yet we find that symbol and metaphor are the very essence of psychoanalysis.

I still deplore Freud's great influence on psychiatry, but not with the fervor of my younger days. As for his followers, I distrust those who glibly answer all questions, who are as certain today as they were yesterday, even though they have changed their dogma, who are organized like a guild or trade union, and who claim to be the victims of persecution when they are few in number, then set about persecuting others when they become powerful.

Because the psychoanalysts have piled absurdity upon absurdity, have violated all the principles of proof, and built curious cults, it may be that I have tended to throw out the good that is in psychoanalysis, the baby, with the foolishness, the dirty water. After all the shouting and tumult die, Freud was a great man, one of the boldest thinkers of all times, and when all is said and done, the fact that he emphasized beyond all others the secret conflicts in men's lives will, in itself, make of him a great figure. Further, he will be remembered as one of those who brought sex out of its hiding-place into the full light of day and helped to make it a permissible topic for scientific and social discussions — something that sorely needed to be done. There is very much dirty water; there is, however, a fine baby, which mankind needs to foster into healthy growth.

A moment for Jung and Adler. Jung laid a useful, even brilliant emphasis on introversion and extroversion, but he gave all his work a mystical slant toward a collective unconsciousness somewhere in the hills of nowhere. Adler gave to psychiatry a very fine term, the "inferiority complex," but I object to its analytic roots. I owe him a great deal, nevertheless, and I think he pointed out one of the great sources of human mental disease.

One tremendous drawback to all the varieties of psychoanalysis is that they have invaded every field of popular discussion and every art. No proof beyond resemblance being necessary, all one has to do is, first, to be quick in discovering resemblance to sex in whatever is said or thought; and this is easy since everything is somewhat straight or somewhat oval. Second, to explain a thing by an assumed formula; for example, a boy loves his mother; therefore he hates his father, is his rival for the mother, and so has an Œdipus complex. Third, to believe that frustration and inhibition are bad, create complexes that are stored in the unconscious, and emerge any number of years later to produce *lasting* disturbances — that is, mental illness. In reality, frustration and inhibition are natural, necessary phenomena and, in normal degrees, condition growth, just as pruning plants does. Fourth, to translate resemblance into identity, such as the immortal Freud himself did on many occasions. A celebrated example is his conclusion that nursing is a sexual act, for does not the flushed and sleepy child, having finished nursing, *resemble* the flushed and sleepy lover, post-coitus? Sensuality is not sexuality, although sexuality is a form of sensuality.

Conjure up a few anthropomorphic entities, which are the lesser and greater gods in the pantheon of psychoanalysis — superego, ego, id, censor, big and little complexes — and you can analyze the quick and the dead with or without seeing them; you can reach the most weighty conclusions about nations, constitutions, heroes, saints, and sinners with or without evidence. Witness the glib way Freud analyzed Moses and Leonardo da Vinci and thus unwittingly proved that a personal psychoanalysis was superfluous.

So we now have newspaper columnists who give advice ex-cathedra on an analytic basis and, in fact, are abetted in the dissemination of their gibberish by psychoanalysts. Religious men make new Trinities with God, Freud, and themselves as the personages. Every day people come into my office to tell me exactly why their relatives (or they themselves) became sick, what complexes they have, the havoc their mothers created in them, and so on, and are scandalized when I tell them that no one as yet knows "causes" in the illness of the patient. There is no end to psychologizing, and the gossips, no longer content with disclosing their neighbors' troubles, can now very glibly explain them. True, the analysts are not to blame for all this, but they have not, in general, acted or talked like scientists. Apparently they need neither statistics nor control studies for what they say.

Great as Freud is, lesser folk do not have to accept him and his doctrines. Great men, as my father once said, have been characterized by the greatness of their mistakes as well as by the greatness of their achievements. Finally, as analysts become more common and as they increase in social power and prestige, they are losing in real conviction, and soon they will be lost in an advancing tide of knowledge. They will not be disproved, but they will become obsolete. So Lecky pointed out that just exactly this process of obsolescence overtook witchcraft.

Although a scientist may and must declare his prejudices, he should also give proof of his impartiality or detachment. My early experiences were such as to turn me strongly toward the faith that truth was essentially the Good. Thus belief and error were objective realities which had, on one side, splendid proponents and, on the other, diabolic opponents. If one saw the error of another man's thinking, one should point it out, lest that falsity of thought imperil mankind and the individual. You get the picture of the confirmed idealist, starry-eyed, with his lance always couched for battle.

Well, I mourn the man that was, but my detachment

is the better for his disappearance. Perhaps an influential, although disliked source of much of my present point of view may be found in Pareto's writings. Of all the cold-blooded cynics who ever walked this earth, the two finest examples come from the Italians, who have, incidentally, furnished a very good proportion of human genius. Machiavelli and Pareto are symbols of detachment from all idealism, and their type of realism hurts as one contemplates it. (For those who want a real exercise in the naked exposition of realism in life, I recommend Pareto's *The Mind and Society;* for readers with less time at their disposal, the ardent synopsis by a great American scientist, Lawrence Henderson, will do very nicely.)

In my work I have never interfered in what I call the "fundamental values" of my patients. Whatever *I* may believe, negatively or positively, about religion, morality, and so on, has nothing to do with the value to my patient of these all-important matters. He may believe what he pleases about God and the angels; and whether he is an orthodox religionist or a complete atheist, I can minister to him without destroying what is essential to his personal stability.

Religion, patriotism, morality of whatever type, economic theory and practice, custom, social habit, and all of the fiercely motivated beliefs of man may be completely dissected into nonlogical, primitive (or superbly evolved) credulity and utterly unproved assertions, yet these may or may not fit human need. The truth of a belief and its usefulness have nothing to do with one another, and the gilded optimism of "The truth shall make you free" contains no precious metal.

I see no evidence that really tells me what truth is, and I know that freedom is strictly limited merely by being part of life. Moreover, the world in places is better faced with "illusions" than with "reality," since some illusions are healthy. Such are, for example, the unproved, unprovable feelings and beliefs that life is worth living, that effort is not futile, that kindness and love are better than cruelty and hate, that reality can be felt, that continuity of existence through the generations makes altruism logical and good. When you dissect a value, you destroy its wholeness, in which reside its worthwhileness and beauty.

In short, there is much to say in favor of nonlogical living, and it may be that *mental health disappears when a man becomes too rational.* I, for one, would not like to see myself as others see me, nor do I care to see the world as it really is. First of all, I would not recognize myself; and secondly, the world might be too horrible to endure.

How many times have I been faced by the question: "Dear doctor, can you tell me what is worth striving for? Why should I live when every second of time ticks off more pain?" My answer has always been: "When health returns, the question will find its own answer. Merely to live with zest is its own reward and its own justification. When you recover, you will rediscover the values that once stood you in good stead, or you will substitute for them other beliefs to buttress you against the corrosion of melancholy."

Mental health as I see it is nonrational. It is not built in rightness or wrongness of belief or the power of the intellect in any way. I have seen mentally sick priests, ministers, rabbis, agnostics, atheists, scientists, doctors, psychiatrists, lawyers, bricklayers, criminals, and housewives; and they have presented practically the same essential depression, delusion, compulsion, and what you will of psychosis and neurosis. I have seen them recover and go back to their old work and ways of life without any very important change in their mode of believing, thinking, and doing. Here, you see, I completely disagree with the popular idea of psychiatry; but ask any experienced psychiatrist, including the psychoanalysts, if all this is not true.

Still, and quite nonrationally, for I have discarded consistency as a life necessity, I find that Jurgen spoke for me after the Brown Man had shown him the Annihilation that lay behind the veil of life:

Yes, you can kill me if you choose, but it is beyond your power to make me believe that there is no justice anywhere, and that I am unimportant. For I would have you know I am a monstrous clever fellow. As for you, you are either a delusion or a god or a degraded Realist. But whatever you are, you have lied to me, and I know that you have lied, and I will not believe in the insignificance of Jurgen. . . . I think there is something in me which will endure. I am fettered by cowardice, I am enfeebled by disastrous memories; and I am maimed by old follies. Still, I seem to detect in myself something which is permanent and rather fine. Underneath everything, and in spite of everything, I really do seem to detect that something. What role that something is to enact after the death of my body, and upon what stage, I cannot guess.

*When fortune knocks I shall open the door. Meanwhile
I will tell you candidly, you brown man, there is something in Jurgen far too admirable for any intelligent ar-
biter ever to fling into the dustheap.*

Jung and William James had no more basis than
Jurgen, the pawnbroker poet, when they posited a consciousness beyond ours, with which we were in communication, which flowed in and out of us, but which was
eternal and gave everlasting values to life.

Some scientists, disheartened by a universe that can
no longer satisfy the deep-set will to believe, have now
supplanted Jove and Jehovah with the idea of a God who
is not absolute but who evolves with man. Scientists
have turned philosophers because the universe is far too
big, and its magnitudes either stun or hurt. For Edding-
ton, God is a mathematician; for Whitehead, He is a
cosmic poet; and while these ideas may give some comfort to them, I find no real sustenance in their pitiful attempts to solve riddles that they themselves say are in-
soluble. Let it go at that — I am willing to let any man
believe what he likes, and he may have consoling faith in
a pantheon or a principle as he pleases. Anybody may
be right where nobody knows, but then nobody knows
who is right.

Some religionists and idealistic philosophers find an
absolute in the mind of man. They speak of MIND in
capitals, as if it were too lofty to have any direct dependence upon the structure of the brain. They believe that
brain events and mind events can never be brought together in a line of cause and effect, that consciousness

always remains a mystery which can never be explained in terms of the chemistry and physics of the body. They feel that considering mind a function of the organism is somehow "gross materialism" and does a great injustice to that noble creature called man. They frown upon the famous statement that mind is as much a function of the brain as the secretion of gastric juice is a function of the stomach.

Man has in his head a "blood-soaked sponge" called a brain, which is his main instrument of knowledge. To that brain come a few sensory avenues by which he can learn about the world. For forty years as a professional neuropsychiatrist, I have dealt with man's brain; I have tested its functions during life and studied it after death chemically, microscopically, and diversely. I marvel at it and respect it, but find it at best a very limited instrument. It lives in an insignificant fragment of the universe and is subject to all kinds of diseases and disasters. Believers in mind seem never to have met an idiot with no more general ideas than a puppy and not so much intelligence. Apparently they never have seen talented men decay into imbecility via old age and cerebral arterial disease; and they never seem to understand that when alcohol enters the human body, chemistry and mind and brain have become knit as finely together as any chain of cause and effect can be in this world of ours.

Every mental disease proclaims that somehow, somewhere, the mind in all the deification that Plato gave to it, in all the abstractions that rob it of its homely realities, is a result and not an entity. Nay, not even a unified result, but many things; and really no boundary can be put to a mental event at the point where it is not physical. I have seen people lose faith, hope, affection, interest, appetite for all of life and love, through illness. I have seen the hero become a coward, the philosopher a cringing fool, the scientist an ignoramus, the passionate lover with all his glow gone, and the wicked sinner apathetically good — while mentally sick. I have seen electric shock, prefrontal lobotomy, benzedrine sulfate, and what you will, restore the qualities that "distinguish man from the beast." Select any quality of mind that you label immanent and transcendental, and I will show you its destruction by disease of the human body.

I can show you people born with but the slightest residue of mind. In every hospital for the feebleminded and epileptic one sees a whole catalogue of misbegotten human beings sans everything that in the eyes of many thinkers somehow makes the human being. It is idle to say that a cretinous idiot has an existent mind that is unable to express itself because the *instrument* of the brain is bogged down by lack of iodine. It is much simpler and more nearly objectively logical to rest with the statement that iodine and brain create mind, even though this solves no final ontological problem.

I may reject the absolutes. Yet sooner or later, in whichever direction my mind travels, it comes to the questions of purpose and consciousness. Thrust them out, however forcibly, through the door, they slink through the window, through the keyhole, more drastically through the chinks and cracks of the scientist himself.

Scientists are men more than they are scientists and

have been human long before they reach the stage of detachment and objectivity that is, in the last analysis, merely the best working attitude for science. As a baby the scientist was attracted by some bright and glittering gewgaw and reached for it. It also happened that he was distressed by some of the objects that came into his little world and finally learned to push these disagreeable things away. So the scientist continues all the rest of his life, reaching and getting, pushing and repelling, though frequently by long, devious, and hidden techniques. Each time the baby who was later to become the scientist got and pushed away, he built up in himself an inexpungeable sense of will, power, and purpose. He felt himself to be a cause, *nolens volens*, a source of power, and he struggled to fulfill some purpose, which in the paradox of development might finally come to be the scientific disestablishment of purpose.

To discard purpose is to throw out will and, with it, responsibility. To discard responsibility is to shove into the limbo of the nonrelevant praise, blame, reward, and punishment, since if there is no will, then neither blame nor praise can logically be distributed. But of those who deny the existence of will, even the most hardened praise and blame others, praise those — for example — who hold the same opinions, blame the recalcitrant ones who stick out for the existence of a will, and glow when praised and are hurt by blame; in fact, they seem to be motivated in part by the desire for praise and the dislike of blame. In all their personal relationships, in their eternal inconsistencies, scientists are men who believe in purpose, or act as if they believed in it, who believe in will and in responsibility, or act as if they did. Thus the life of every man who is a scientist is divided into two parts; in the one as a scientist he is objective and discards purpose; and in the other, as a man, he acts entirely differently and thus becomes at least two different persons.

I once asked a great physicist to develop a camera of unique properties. "This camera," I said, "is to build *itself*, not out of steel and glass and rubber and the like, but, let us say, out of cereals, meats, grain, sugar, oxygen, vitamin A, and diverse substances. It will start out undifferentiated and grow in size and complexity until it has developed shutters, lenses, a photoreactive surface, and it not only will take pictures continually, but will remember them somehow, and then, to cap a climax, give them meaning. Moreover, it must be able to repair itself and to guard itself from harm; and finally, it is to have a way, by means of curious mechanisms, of breeding itself, starting microscopically and growing to visible size and complicated function in another creature. These and many other specifications are to be brought to functional and structural reality in your project." At this point the physicist, restraining his great wrath, exclaimed: "You are asking me to make an eye! I can develop a camera that will do some things the eye cannot do, but of course I cannot make an eye."

If the physicist has purpose, every cell in his body, being a better physicist in most ways than he is, may also claim purpose, unless purpose is made equivalent to consciousness. If purpose means choosing means to an end — not a final end, but a goal — then every cell of the body and certainly every organism have purpose, unless there is no purpose anywhere. If there is not, I cannot write about it; you cannot think about it; and the discussion ends. But if there is such a concept embodied in a word, then every cell in every body has purpose. Now, that does not mean ultimate purpose and purposer, but it allows room for that comfort necessary to most people who reject orthodoxy, that this is a universe striving for some goal. For some, this is " base materialism"; for me, it is a working credo. Such a disagreement might disturb me if I did not have any inconsistencies to fall back on.

I wish I could quote exactly the first Oliver Wendell Holmes, a man I admire with affection because he was a doctor and a good Bostonian with a lively wit, a penetrating mind, and the ability to speak and write with charm and wisdom. He says that each man goes to the ocean of knowledge with a little tin cup that he is to fill with his quota of wisdom and understanding. However learned he may be, the world of learning has become so extended in a thousand special directions that he really knows little, since wisdom is not bought in the marketplaces, nor is it necessarily acquired by a long life of work in any human field. This book is my tin cup — that, and only that.

CHAPTER III

THE GREAT UNLEARNING

*"And the children suspect nothing and reach the
age of life with a bandage over their eyes
and reason — without suspecting what the
under side of existence means — without
knowing that people do not think as they
speak, do not talk as they act — without
knowing that one must live in a state of
continual warfare or at best of armed
peace, with everybody — without ever im-
agining that one is always sure to be
tricked if one is simple, deceived if one is
sincere, maltreated if one is kind and good.*

*"Some go on to the moment of their
death in this blindness of loyalty, honor,
and probity — being so thoroughly upright
that nothing can open their eyes.*

*"Others, ultimately disabused, yet un-
able to understand, are perpetually stum-
bling here and there in wild desperation;
and die at last in the belief that they have
been the sport of exceptional ill fortune."*
(*Maupassant: "Forgiveness"*)

SOONER or later the alert-minded youngster in our civilization discovers that his elders have indoctrinated him
with a distorted, partial, and devitalized view of life and

formed a great conspiracy to prevent and pervert a full view of the facts of life (and I do not mean by this merely the bees and butterfly learning of sex). There then begins the great unlearning, which may be followed by the great relearning or may not, since few go beyond a close-mouthed and hidden cynicism created by their disillusionment. To many it comes as a great shock to learn that parents may be unfaithful to each other, cruel, stupid, and utterly unworthy of the respect and honor that is enjoined upon each child by all of the great religions of the world; that grown-ups in general are a sad lot, quite definitely and piously pointing out one way of life to their children and secretly living another, and that few of them know anything thoroughly beyond their own little bread-and-butter learning.

The children eventually realize that the mother is not at all beautiful, or if she makes a good appearance, it is by a painfully assiduous technique. Moreover, they discover that pettiness, jealousy, and neurosis are not at all uncommon in the mother they are supposed to revere. They learn that the father is not the great man; in fact, that he usually is a little man, not particularly strong, often foolishly despotic and easily hoodwinked, certainly not important.

But this is not the most of the great unlearning. "You find," said one very acute boy to me, "that you are supposed to put your brains in your pocket about many of the things of life, about sex and marriage and parenthood — that even to think about them would be enough to destroy all your values. . . . You learn that religion is to be believed in without question. . . . You find that politics and politicians are crooked, that you really cannot trust anybody. Then you are supposed to believe in the patriots of yesterday, although debunkers show you that the patriots of one era are the politicians of an earlier one. . . . Whenever you strip off disguises, you find that everyone wears masks, everyone fakes and struts and lies in some degree, little or great. You do yourself, to your surprise. And then, to cap the absurd climax, you know that when you grow up, you'll lie to your own children about the real nature of man and the world."

I grant that this boy was direct in his powers of speech and exceptionally frank and bitter in his reactions to the great falsity, which was his term after he heard about the great unlearning. But less articulate young people find the unlearning no less destructive.

In some groups boys and girls learn with shock, relatively late in life, of what is deliberately hidden in our civilization. Many of the popular books to initiate the young have been of the "birds and bees" type. They teach the child the words, but leave out the music of this cacophonic symphony and so are only feebly preparatory for maturity. Written words of warning are as nothing against the sudden meeting of eyes, a casual contact of thighs, or the pulsating passion of two young bodies clasped together, let us say, in the permitted dance. And because of the strong forces against the enlightenment of children, even these feeble books do not reach the vast majority of the young in our culture. Most children learn what they can by stray hints or quick revealing glimpses of the hidden sexual life, perhaps by a stark example from the animal world, or occasionally through little orgies of revelation and experiment.

You can get some idea of the hidden when you read the anthropologists' account of the lives of children in what we call aboriginal societies. Consider the writings of Malinowski and Margaret Mead, to cite only two of a busy and indicative group. Early the savage child sees birth and death, and he grows up in the nakedness and viscerality of these initiating and terminal events which our children view rarely, if ever, in their stark reality. The organs of sex are no palpitating mystery to the savage child, and it is hard to see how romantic and lyrical sexuality could arise to falsify the actualities in Samoa or among the Australian groups. For them clothes, while they may beautify, do not hide or mystify life, and animality, which is basic in man as in all other creatures, is not a hideous and reproachful thing, since excretion and copulation are relatively public and not particularly obscene. Virginity is no goddess, and the final experiences of sex are not deferred and forbidden, while the exciting and preparatory forepleasures are extolled and practiced.

The romantic era in sex is a recent event in the history of the man-woman difficulty, and so it is only in our civilization that unlearning in sex, love, and marriage has become important. The ecstatic expectations of living on love and kisses are roughly shattered by the shocking discovery that the Beautiful Woman has troublesome bodily organs and functions (has viscera and is visceral, to use biological terms) and needs much technique to be mysterious and charming, while the Virile Man is only so at times and at other times is so-so. Too much has been expected because of the conspiracy of popular novels, plays, and love songs, and too little has been known because of moral codes. In almost no department of our early lives is there so much false direction, misinformation, and invalid expectation as in sex, love, and marriage. The amount of relearning necessary so taxes physical endurance, emotional stability, and mental integrity as to be a favorite explanation for mental disorder and social unhappiness.

The stresses of our civilization become more pressing as we go from nakedness to ceremonious and conventional clothing, from animal to human social living. We teach the child to hide the animal in him. This is the basis of manners and morals; this accounts for the development of the obscene and the vile, asceticism and holiness. Its development has created the world, the flesh, and the Devil, and it underlies all the notions of that trinity. All these and many other matters to come up relate to this struggle against the animal, which Freud would call the battle between the id and the ego and the superego, which St. Augustine would label the struggle between God and the Devil, which a Puritan in reverse — like D. H. Lawrence — would stigmatize as the conflict between the mystic dark good and the arid morality.

There are some who are too conventional, too timid, or too stupid to see the contradictions between life as taught and life as it is. There are those who are crushed or torn asunder. There are those who give lip homage and outward deference, but live secret lives with their tongues in their cheeks. There are those who suffer from disharmonies in one or more fields, as when acquisitiveness finds reasonable scope, but sex is the great problem, or vice versa. As Aldous Huxley wisely said in the brilliant days of *Point Counter Point*, there are as many perversions of the acquisitive impulses as of the sexual. And there are those who reach a reasonable compromise, with wisdom as the main keynote of their lives.

The great unlearning may not even be clearly conscious. It may be so hidden in the survival pattern of actions as not even to be perceived. We see it in the father who reproves his son for stealing an apple, but cheats on his income tax and sees no inconsistency between his stern disapproval of his son and his smug approval of himself. The codes of life by which men govern their actions are, in short, declared and hidden at one and the same time. The disharmonies may be cynically expressed or felt with guilt and dismay. Authority arises to work out codes, which become enthroned. Hypocrisy acknowledges morality, but works in disguises and under cover; crime circumvents and defies; and endless modifications of reaction take place as the unlearning is followed in greater or lesser degree by the relearning.

All this has been said in a thousand and one ways by pessimists, cynics, and realists. It has been said very well by the author of *The Natural History of Nonsense*, Bergen Evans:

Mice and men are alike in this respect, and modern society sometimes looks as if it were deliberately designed by some fiendish experimenter in order to drive us insane. We are brought up to expect rewards for certain

*kinds of behavior and then thrown into a world in which
none of the signals works. We are taught as children to
be kind, self-sacrificing, and helpful, never to be greedy
or aggressive. Then we must live in a ruthlessly competitive economy. We are taught to be honest, in preparation
for a world in which honesty is often penalized and dis-
honesty, in a thousand forms, is often rewarded. Our
ambition is stimulated and we are assured of success if
we will only "apply ourselves," when actually, by the
very nature of things, nine out of ten must be disappointed, and chance carries as much weight as merit.*

*The result is mass frustration and despair. Only the
stoical and the cynical can preserve a measure of stability; yet stoicism is the wisdom of madness and cynicism
the madness of wisdom. So none escapes.*

This is really a statement of the experimental production of mental disease in animals, one of the great
achievements of the Russian Pavlov.

Do we need, does mankind need, to be trained by
priests and pundits, to be conditioned in our early childhood into the great expectation that becomes for most
the great frustration? In part we must discipline and disguise our native desires, because unvarnished life is not
worth living despite its "naturalness," and there is an
artistic trend to civilized living and believing which is a
reason for being. The road from the tree-dwellers, our
ancestors, has been a painful one, but we cannot go back.
We must find ways to develop our powers and yet not
crucify the aboriginal who is the main reality within us.
I believe this double process of development is possible

to us. Otherwise we are in this dilemma: if we over-emphasize the animal, we live in a world bereft of beauty, order, and disciplined achievement; if we crush the animal, we destroy the basis of desire and satisfaction, health and endurance, and make human development so one-sided as to fall into despair.

Chapter IV

THE LOW-DOWN ON AUTHORITIES, INCLUDING PSYCHIATRISTS

In my day I have lectured a great deal both as a professional teacher in medical schools and as a so-called "popular lecturer" to lay audiences. During one of my earliest adventures in the somewhat comic role of "speaker at a Women's Club," when I was sandwiched in between "The Modern Dance" and "Vitamins," I was suddenly assailed by a demoralizing fantasy. It was that the faces turned toward the platform were those of monkeys listening gravely and uncritically as I, another monkey, spouted forth — what? How did it come about that I had become an "authority" in fields of such importance and such vagueness as mental health, emotional control, and child-rearing, not to speak of the mental diseases? Neither then nor now have these subjects reached that definiteness which is necessary for popular discussion. *Mea culpa!*

So what is authority? To say that I know how authority arises would be to set myself up as an authority on authority, which I am not. True, I have read almost all that has been written on the subject, but much is nonsense, a good deal is itself unjustified authoritarianism, and the rest is — interesting reading. So with due modesty I shall give one partial answer to that question.

Perhaps one of the best answers is given by that hard-boiled American sociologist A. G. Keller, who, as the successor to the even more tough William Graham Sumner, author of *Folkways*, has carried on a tradition of uncompromising realism:

If human history is a tangled drama, its plot, at least, is simple: "Man faces The Awkward Situation." The cavedweller rounds a corner and runs into a saber-toothed tiger; the modern nation encounters the liquor issue as a lion in its path. And the first line of man's speaking part has always been:

Man (anxiously) "Now what to do?"

Men have wanted to be told what to do *— not what to think. Later, perhaps, what to think, if there is time. Thinking is hard, especially when weary with the day's work; it is thankfully turned over to someone else. Men have wanted only to be happy, in a simple, human way; always they have prayed for health, food enough, and offspring. They have ever been willing to fall in behind any guide who proclaimed impressively enough that he could lead them to their heart's desire, and glad to pay him liberally for his services. Under the circumstances there has been no lack of seers who, overcoming a shrinking modesty, have made known their competence to size up any and all situations and to lead unerringly away from mischance toward security.*

Seers and Seers

The guide most favored by mankind has been the medicine-man, or priest, reputed to have direct access to di-

vine wisdom; and in his wake came along presently the philosopher who, sinking a shaft into his own mighty mind, and prospecting and introspecting through its darksome galleries, emerged with Absolutes infallible to the good life: Truth, Beauty, Duty, Faith, Loyalty. The philosopher has never seriously crowded his predecessor in popularity, because he could never tell people, in a few plain, loud words, what to do. Besides, philosophers have talked a mysterious jargon and each has contradicted the other. When the old-time priest rumbled out of his beard: "Thus saith the Lord! Fetch a goat!" that was something any clod could understand and carry in his mind. He hurried off to get the goat. The Unapproachable One was going to descend from on high and graciously eat the goat. When a perplexed soul is told: "Be thou loyal to Loyalty!" he goes away feeling much as if he had been fed on shadow-broth. If he can, he sticks to the elder, lusty, hearty, comprehensible gods; if not, he makes the best of his confusion and resigns himself to meeting his fate under his own steam, and as it comes, instead of hoping to be told how to head off calamity as a whole and at its source.[1]

Man's need for help comes from the very construction of the human being. He is assailed by many and often contradictory stimuli, and he has only a relatively few ways of reacting. Therefore the very troublesome and dangerous matter of choice and choosing is thrust upon him, although he has no desire to choose and very little

[1] A. G. Keller: *Man's Rough Road* (Frederick A. Stokes Co. and Yale University Press, 1932), pp. 3–4.

real knowledge to guide him. The relevant knowledge may be ten thousand years away, and obviously he cannot wait that long.

Consider a very simple situation. A savage, desperately hungry and driven to foraging in the forest, comes upon a new fruit hanging quite temptingly from the low limb of a tree. It is red and pretty (visual stimulus); it feels smooth and satiny (tactile stimulus); its smell is unfamiliar and somewhat disagreeable (olfactory stimulus). Shall he pluck it or leave it where it is? He remembers being made sick in the past by strange fruit (guiding memory) and were he not desperately hungry (present primitive urgency), he could readily make up his mind to walk away and await more certain and safe food. He cannot tear himself away (immediate desire), and yet he fears to take it (past and future combined). He has only one motor outlet, a pair of hands, but many competing and contradictory sensory pathways and memories for the use of those hands. Moreover, the matter may be further complicated by an utterly devastating (and entirely irrelevant) moral issue: it is the middle of the day and he has been enjoined by priests and chiefs that he must not eat at that time. (Many of our present-day injunctions make no more sense.)

While he is beset by doubt, along comes an old man. The old man knows no more about the fruit than he does. But the old man is an authority, and he says: "Eat, my friend, and give me a part as my fee." The savage has cried out: "Help, help!" and Authority, in the familiar form of the old man (ancestors, Fathers of the Republic, senators), has answered that eternal cry by assuming responsibility for the selection from competing ways of conduct. The authority speaks, not necessarily in accordance with any facts, but according to the time, the cultural custom, the caste or group pressure. If he turns out to be "wrong," a "reason" can always be found for the failure, in terms of the savage's lack of faith (or, in Freudian terms, his great resistance to something or other) or some past sin of his own or of his kin.

The contradictions in life force choice, since the ways of reaction are always fewer than the competing stimuli. The dog who simultaneously barks and wags his tail presents a dilemma in conduct. Which end is one to believe? Should one fight the barker or pat the wagger?

The problem of choice becomes more complicated and pressing when biological drive meets social inhibition, a matter that is the very heart of man's dilemmas, and causes far more turmoil within poor Homo than the more direct question of whether or not to eat the fruit. By a fantastic and yet necessary quirk of his nature, man long ago reached the point where he declared the most natural acts vile, obscene, immoral, and wrong. Yet his bodily structures seemingly know nothing of this teaching and preaching, because they date back millions of years before any teaching and preaching took place at all.

There is an evocative principle in human life. The cry for "Help! Help!" evokes in some people the urge to advise and govern the action of others. To teach and direct is as innate in man as to cry out for help and direction. The more ignorant the authority, the more dogmatic it is. In the fields where no real knowledge is even possible, the authorities are the fiercest and most assured and pun-

ish non-belief with the severest of penalties. The more
vociferously certain an authority is, the more he is believed. Since credulity arises before skepticism, and since
men desperately seek security, the men who try to be
reasonable, to assemble facts for and against any way of
life, to reach conclusions slowly and diffidently, are not
followed by the mass. But proclaim any absurdity loudly
enough, repeat it fiercely, avoid reason and discussion,
use satire, threats, mockery, enjoin in the name of the
good, and true, and the beautiful, promise much and without equivocation, and you will be followed to the death.
So great is the hunger of man for the certainties of "what
to do," "what to say," and "what to believe."

Thus authorities arise in every field. For example,
despite religion, despite the teaching of immortality, despite the fanning of men into fanatic frenzies that dis-
regarded death, despite the heroism that illuminates the
private and the public records of mankind, the fear of
death has never been greatly lessened or markedly influenced by any manner of propaganda. Man has always
wanted to know how to avoid sickness and death; and
other men have arisen to direct him. At first they used
magic. Later they divided man into four humors. Gradually the bold and unorthodox among them started dissection, built up faculties and hospitals, and slowly emanci-
pated themselves from religion, dogmatism, logical de-
duction, and abstract principles. Painfully they passed
from magic to empiricism, and then they entered science,
collaborating with physicists, chemists, biologists, psychologists, and sociologists. The thermometer measures
heat; the microscope adds a thousandfold eye; X-rays

penetrate into the recesses of the organism; mathematics and electricity and, most importantly, the scientific spirit and technique enter to answer the cry for help. The authorities — that is, shaman, medicine man, doctor — filled with crass error, pomposity, and the stupid and false ethics of professionalism, have thus passed along a bloody road. Yet, with all its bitter faults, with all its falsity, with all the positive hurt to human health and happiness, authority has to be, because even if failure comes, men need the comforting feeling of "Well, we did our best."

Today we have "popular authorities" on the "newest" ideas of health and disease. Each newspaper and weekly news magazine has a health column; on the radio carefully selected medical men tell when to consult the doctor about the little lump in the breast or the loss of breath after slight exertion. Fear of illness, which is really fear of death, evokes the now endless flow of publications and publicity releases on How to Be Healthy and Avoid Disease, When to See Your Doctor, How to Stop Worrying, How to Detect Cancer, How to Avoid Heart Disease, and What to Eat. While it is true that the current information on diet has been of some benefit, particularly as far as obesity is concerned, the pleasure of eating has diminished to the point of a huge injury to appetite itself. Increasing resistance by taking vitamins is still a bonanza for the drug-manufacturers, but increased resistance is not obtained by increasing vitamins. In the virus diseases, in fact, an excessive or even a high level of certain vitamins lowers resistance just because the virus thrives on a high vitamin level and dies of starvation if the vitamin content of the body is low. This is also the case in malaria. So there is evidence that the apparent common-sense dictum "Raise your nutrition level for better vitality" happens to be wrong.

The general worship of health has introduced a health-consciousness, which finally becomes anxiety, the worst disease of the mind. The anxiety increases with "enlight-enment" and has become so widespread that it may now be called "social hypochondriasis." When any popular exposition of headache stresses the relationship to brain tumor and brain pathology, doctors' offices, clinics, and hospitals are flooded with a new group of patients. The headache is magnified, slight giddiness becomes dizziness, and all the mentioned symptoms are presented. For the patient with a fear of brain tumor all the good has gone from life. Most of the dreaded anxiety-states start as fear of illness based on heightened introversion and the grim tendency of the body to enact symptoms according to fear.

Moreover, what doctors say today they may unsay to-morrow. A man who suffered from prolonged and sonor-ous belching consulted an eminent specialist. The doctor made the appropriate examinations, prescribed a powder for the patient to take before meals and a capsule after meals, and advised him above all to drink no water with his meals. Some six months later the patient returned, claiming timidly that his belching was still as chronic and noisy as ever. Examination was repeated; the same powder and capsules were dispensed; then the doctor advised: "Drink plenty of water with your meals." The astounded patient could not refrain from saying: "But, doctor, six months ago you told me to drink no water with my meals." The great man looked him over with a gracious and pitying glance. "Ah," said he, "science makes great strides these days!"

There are fashions, ever changing, in medical belief. It is quite amusing to read the title of a new book, *Hypnosis Comes of Age.* Hypnosis is older than anesthesia, asepsis, and antisepsis, the bacterial theory of disease, psychoanalysis, the knowledge of vitamins, and, in fact, all of modern medicine. An old teacher of mine once said: "Hypnosis is like the proverbial woman of the streets — every so often she becomes respectable, but soon relapses into her old status."

Still the cry for security from disease and death, the needs and whims of man, and even hostile chance breed authorities who say confidently: "Do this and that, and do not do the other." Authorities finally get together in trade associations, build up professions, shroud themselves in mystery and make-believe, partly genuine and partly fake, and finally create great institutions that exert deep and directing social pressure and become our social heritage.

The plight of man in every nook and corner of his world of time and space, in seeking and choosing his food, quenching his thirst, copulating with his woman, living with his fellows, tilling the soil, hunting and seeking God and gods, speaking properly, dressing as he should, developing a fine leg, using the right fork, and wiping his nose *à la mode*, caused him to create all the forces of teaching, preaching, leading, fooling, faking. It is need and credulity that evoke dogmatic precepts. It is submission that evokes force, and passivity that evokes domination. Suffering may and does indeed evoke help and pity as well as cruelty; ignorance may evoke kindly teaching as well as deception; sickness finally evokes humanitarianism and medical research as well as quackery and deceit. Laws may spring from harshness and the will to dominate, but injustice also evokes the reforming spirit and the determined attack on inequity. It is my hope, as it is that of every ardent worker in humane fields, that some day human need will evoke a combined trinity of Science, Goodwill, and Wisdom to make living worth while. Meanwhile authority at least gives poor Homo the safe, the right, the proper, the face-saving, the adequate thing-to-do and thing-to-believe, the knowledge of how to act so that he will not be rejected by his group.

Yet there are those who are strong enough to live precariously — that is, without absolute authority. How are they to choose when and what to follow? Are there any criteria to distinguish between true and false authoritarianism, to know the real from the shoddy, science from quackery? When absolutes are involved, as in religion and philosophy, I am no guide, but I can say that the more a belief is made a matter of right and wrong, the more fiercely divergence and skepticism are denounced, the less the dogma is to be believed and followed. This is, of course, only a general rule and applies to articles of belief and not to legal conduct. Murder and thievery are universally denounced and, at present, even the skeptic should not kill outside of the permitted bounds or steal in unorthodox ways. There are, as you must know, right and wrong ways of killing and taking.

Where absolutes are not involved, there are some good rules to follow, even though the full truth is never known and all rightness is merely relevant and temporary. In the first place, the more an authority depends on slogans involving emotion, or pious generalities, and the more partisan he is, the less he is to be believed. Whether the slogan is virtue, morality, holiness, or patriotism makes no difference; the wise reader will avoid devotees of any slogans.

Secondly, the more an authority invokes the "good old days" in whatever field, the less he is to be followed by the reasonable. There are no good old days nor even old days; preceding days were merely younger days, just as you were younger once than you are now. The implication of wisdom and goodness in the past is the silliest and yet the most compelling of paradoxes. Bad as these days are, there were in former days crueler punishment for all crimes and so-called crimes, more slavery, and less knowledge. The only past we know about was based on ignorance and the harshest cruelty. Even the great thinkers, with few exceptions, are remarkable because they lived in so ignorant a world. At any rate, when an authority harks back to the sages of yore, show him the door.

Finally, do not be misled by the fallacy of the positive instance, which really means watch out for the great god Coincidence. A clock that stands entirely still is "right" by coincidence twice a day. If you deal with a disease that in general tends toward recovery, then whatever you do short of actual injury, and including prayers, spells, holy phrases, and the laying on of hands, as well as elixirs, drugs, and X-ray, may "cure" (that is, coincide with spontaneous cure). This has been the chief factor in the reputation of healers of all sorts, including the regular members of the profession. With any variable state, improvement may take place at any time and according to unknown laws. Unless a man cites his failures, and unless he uses the technique of the "control study," you need not believe him. If there were not a condition called hysteria, which looks very serious but is in reality "curable" by any hocus-pocus that impresses the patient, there would be no miraculous healings to impress the credulous and there might be no great religious leaders. One Greek cynic, when he saw the great piles of crutches in a certain Temple of Healing, said: "Just *one* wooden leg would be better." Or, say I: "one set of false teeth or a glass eye." Evidently God can cure cancer and tuberculosis, but cannot grow a new leg, a new set of teeth, or a new eye. This is blasphemy, but not mine — the priests and faith healers are guilty of limiting God's powers.

During World War II the most amusing demonstration of human credulity was the respect and attention paid to military commentators. Not one was ever right beyond the law of chance, beyond the formula that if he talked enough, he was bound to be right occasionally. The favorite and face-saving method of some of these gentlemen, who were apparently made of brass and with gall to the nth power of infinity, was in essence: "The Russians may win this battle, but of course they may lose if it is not a stalemate." Yet people glued their ears to the radio to listen to these self-styled authorities and quoted them assiduously. A literate child would have had as good a batting average in prognostication or even in understanding the significance of the events they recorded, yet their errors were forgotten and the occasional bull's-eye marveled over.

Recently the stock market dropped, and the next day the authorities were divided into three camps: those who said it was only a temporary recession due to this and that, those who said it would go down further owing to that and this, and a few candid souls who said nobody knows anything about the stock market. All of these, however, will continue to pose and be followed as authorities.

To understand any situation where many variable factors exist, one must have extensive control studies and well-organized experiments covering a long period of time. Since one cannot truly experiment with human social affairs and since control studies are impossible, there can be no real authorities on such subjects as economics. Even the most learned, hard-working, and earnest economists are swayed by their convictions, by preconceived notions of good and evil, and few of them feel free to express themselves with complete candor. In this country most economists feel that they must abide by the shibboleths of democracy and free enterprise, just as in Russia the dogma of Communism and the Rights of the Proletariat rule the minds of the experts.

Then what is valid authority, and where do we find it? Honest statistics, where they are applicable, separate the valid from the invalid. One does not discover new drugs, new machines, and the eternal verities by statistics, nor does one know *why* some people live longer than others by statistical studies, although one can say that in general lean people live longer than fat ones. That is all one can say by statistics alone, since here figures and statistics have to be separated. Whenever there is much material to be analyzed before anything can be solidly established as a probability, one may depend on the following principles:

The figures must represent a fair sample of the field covered. Remember what happened to the *Literary Digest* poll because the sample was of people who were "naturally" Republicans and omitted the potential Democrats?

The matters analyzed must be of the same nature. You cannot make good hamburger by putting overalls, beef, onions, and snowballs through the best meat-grinder. For example, in eugenical statistics, especially in the past, such social matters as crime, such gossipy matters as sex delinquency, such environmental conditions as brain injury, such unknowns as cancer, were put into the same hopper with feeblemindedness. And lo, we had the entirely fallacious studies about the Kallikaks and the other "royal" families of the feebleminded.

To cite a few cases where the variable factors are many is of no importance. You can play bridge every night for a month and get marvelous hands or the worst ever and thus develop ideas of grandeur or of persecution. If you play for a year, the luck will generally average out. I take very little stock in the greatness of a baseball team on the basis of the number of games played, even in a season. That number is not enough for real relative evaluation, since injuries, sickness, the fallacies of umpires, the way a wife is behaving, and the great god Coincidence, named by the sports writers the "breaks," are too prevalent to be ruled out by one hundred and fifty-four games. And a prophet has to guess right more than a dozen times for me to pay any attention to him.

I am now reading for review *The Reach of the Mind* by Professor Rhine of Duke University. This is an experimental study of telepathy, clairvoyance, and kindred phenomena. The subject of the experiment tries to "reach out with his mind" and call the correct card which has been read by someone else, or "influence" cast dice into a certain pattern. For several years experiments have been carried on to see whether or not the number of times in which this is accomplished exceeds the laws of chance. Is the material of this book a valid proof of these "psychical phenomena"? In connection with proof, Rhine makes many errors, which I may as well elaborate. Such a clinical study may help us answer the question: whom shall we believe and why (or why not)?

First, it is obvious that Dr. Rhine believed what he "found" before he experimented. This does not rule out the truth or believability of his conclusions, but makes us extra cautious, since the will to believe is very dangerous to objectivity and truth. We all know that, or should.

Second, he has a very curious way of reaching conclusions. He gets very excited about those subjects who guess or influence a correct answer beyond the laws of chance, since this proves the existence of ESP (extrasensory perception). *But when the same subject does badly*, he excuses the failure because, forsooth, the psychic power is exhausted or the mere effect of the scientific precaution hampered the semidivine effluvium. It is heads I win and tails you lose with Dr. Rhine, which is the way most seers, prophets, and mystics work.

Third, he is very credulous about such matters as the foreseeing of future events. He cites the positive instance of the lady who foresees her husband's death in a distant place and then gets a telegram announcing its occurrence at the very time she got this peek into the veiled future. But he limits his statistical researches to cards, dice, and the like and makes no effort to find out how many distraught people have foreseen disasters never delivered out of the womb of time. The acceptance of the fallacy of the positive instance stamps this work as utterly unscientific.

There is a very pertinent question we may ask ourselves in respect to the credibility of any authority or any preacher of a doctrine, which is: in what social climate would he be believed? The further one goes into illiteracy, superstition, and the past ages, the more telepathy and clairvoyance are taken for granted as natural phenomena. If an authority's dicta are more in accordance with credulity than objectivity, if he would more easily be believed by the centuries before the Renaissance than after it, if shopgirls believe him and scholars reject him, you are safe — that is, reasonably safe — in disbelief. In general, ideas, beliefs, and dogmas, like men, may be judged by the company they keep.

Well, how about popular psychology and psychiatry, and what to believe in these expanding fields? It is well to remember that in all science and especially in medicine the optimists write by far the most, since pessimism does not pay dividends or royalty checks. There are few people interested in abstract truth, but many who seek relief from pain, doubt, inferiority, and the concrete ills of life. One writer had the smallest of audiences for a book on human stupidity, but engaged the attention of the whole country with a best-seller on how life begins at an age when it really starts declining.

The popular books on psychology are almost all extremely fallacious, not only in their optimism, but also in their expressed (and unexpressed) certainty of knowledge. There are psychiatrists and near-psychiatrists who speak as if they had become the new agents of God, and claim that they can furnish principles sure-proof against illness and despair. One writer says that if you know "how to relax," you will be all right mentally, which is like saying that if you gargle a mouth-wash, you will cure sore throat, pneumonia, and cancer. Besides, in most mental illnesses the capacity to relax is as much impaired as the integrity of a bone is destroyed by fracture. Another man proclaims the *value* of the orgasm and has become the god of a very interesting cult, with little clusters of believers all the way from California to New York. Yet no one other than the author has seen the Orgone, a blue something that is the basis of orgasm, neurosis, psychosis, storms at sea, and star clusters. Other authorities rush into print and into lecture halls to tell mothers that they must avoid "traumatic weaning and traumatic toilet training" if they are to prevent the neurosis and psychosis of the future generation; and they speak with all the definiteness that only a world of statistics collected for a hundred years could justify. It is one thing to cure the sick; it is quite another to be the newest bearers of truth and enlightenment. At any rate, I have seen the therapies come and the therapies go; and I have seen writers labeled as geniuses by the lay press while the medical press snickered. Now and then the community may hail a great man whom the elect refuse to recognize, but not in science, even though this is a favorite theme for romantic movies. Science may make many mistakes in acclaiming great men, but the common man has no discrimination whatever.

There is a tendency today to put the psychiatrist in the place of priest as absolute authority. I know most of the distinguished psychiatrists of America, and the distribution of wisdom and wise living among them is about equal to that in the general population. As one reads the articles that appear either in the popular journals or in those books meant for the layman, one would never guess that the following is the actual state of psychiatry at the present time:

Only a few diseases are really understood as to cause, and these are the result of bodily changes of definite types. Among these are syphilis, alcoholism, vitamin deficiency, old age, with its arterial degeneration and structural alteration, and a few scattered organic diseases such as brain tumor and Alzheimer's disease.

In the causation of the rest, only theory, prepossession, and prejudice reign supreme, without proof. Some writers, like myself, lay emphasis on inborn heredity, although without any knowledge of how that heredity works or of what the hereditary change may be. Others speak of psychological causation in terms of Freud, Jung, or Adler, the simple psychobiology of Meyer, or the newer, rapidly developing varieties of modified psychoanalysis, such as those of Alexander, Horney, and Masserman. All of these writers are persuasive and dogmatic, and go so far beyond the evidence as to be unscientific. Although psychologizing is a very alluring mental exercise, even the simplest neurosis is not understood in any complete way, and some utterly unknown factor (or factors) is probably causative.

Moreover, and this is all-important, there is more humbug or misinformation about the cure of mental disease than about the causation. There have been advances; slowly progress appears on the scene; and I have faith that science will some day "cure" all mental disease. But not right away. Anyway, I shall say this: that the major mental diseases, the psychoses, are not in the least curable by psychotherapeutics, including psychoanalysis. Many of these diseases are favorably *influenced* by insulin coma, electric shock, and prefrontal lobotomy, but they are not cured in any final sense at all, although the therapeutic situation has become much more hopeful.

The same is true of those mysterious diseases called the neuroses. There is great help in the personal influence of the doctor, in some drugs, in physical and vocational re-education, in the change of emotional attitude *if* it can be brought about. There may be and there is some value in prayer, psychoanalysis, and hypnosis. The most important factor is time, the great healer. Either the patient dies of an intercurrent disease, or he gets well of himself, or he gives up doctors and learns to live with his illness, as a man lives with a shrew by shrugging his shoulders and keeping his mouth shut.

I think of myself as a sort of glorified plumber. A plumber called in because water was splashing on the dining-room floor would examine the pipes and might find a little hole "due" to rust. That is, the "cause" of the leak was rust. He might discuss the nature of water, oxidation, and iron, and soon he would be away from that leak into the ions and emanations of the whole universe. He might continue indefinitely linking time, space, matter, and what you will with that leak, and finally decide with Hume that all one could ever say about any event was its antecedence, or sequence, or coincidence to or with other events. Still, without knowing why there should be rust in this particular pipe, he could remove the faulty section, galvanize another piece, put it where it belonged, and stop the leak.

And so, to end our section on authorities:

Believe, if you must, to be comfortable mentally. Alas, the tempo changes so rapidly nowadays in all things, including faith, that in order to be fashionable you will have to change your beliefs as you do your garments. If you are hardy and skeptical, keep in mind that there are some ways of guessing what is relatively true and what is palpably false.

Chapter V

WOMAN, THE AUTHORITIES' SCAPEGOAT

My father said that the Angel of Death, in his peregrinations through the world, came to the bedside of a young and beautiful woman with whom he fell in love. Instead of consigning her to the tomb, he took her to his subterranean abode and married her. In the course of time they had a son, who became the most important doctor in the world. The secret of his great reputation lay in a completely reliable but hitherto unknown clinical sign. When he came into a sickroom, if the patient was to die, the doctor would see his father, invisible to others, standing triumphantly at the head of the bed; if the patient was to live, the Angel of Death was standing rather gloomily at the foot. Therefore the doctor's prognoses were infallible. When he said of the most desperate case: "This patient is going to live," his prescription and treatment were given credit, as is the case with doctors. If the patients were inevitably to die, he would say: "Call someone else. I can do nothing for this sufferer."

On one occasion he was called to the bedside of a very beautiful young girl and promptly fell in love with her. Although his father stood at the head of the bed, he said: "This patient is going to live." His invisible father shook his head violently to indicate that this was not so. The doctor repeated the prognosis, firmly and bravely looking his father directly in the eye. The next day the son again appeared at the bedside, and lo, his father was still standing at the head of the bed. "This patient," repeated the doctor resolutely, "is going to live." His father nearly shook his head off. The doctor went home and spoke to his mother. He told her that his father was denying him the one thing he wanted of life. His mother nodded ominously. The next day when the doctor visited the patient, lo and behold, his father was standing sheepishly with head bowed at the foot of the bed.

"Such," said my father, "has been the power of woman from time immemorial."

And so it has! Yet, paradoxically enough, the official position of woman has always been that of an inferior.

Only by inference do we know of the social position of primitive woman. Very likely there was little sentiment and woman-worship in the earliest days. Female *Homo sapiens* probably was strong and enduring, though undoubtedly of lesser physical strength than her mate, a fact that together with her recurrent helplessness in pregnancy both evoked his protection and gave him the place of superiority and power.

Most likely it has been a man's world from the very beginning. Even in the so-called matriarchal societies, where the woman's name and kinship go to the child and where her husband seems to be a social fifth wheel, it is another male, the maternal uncle of the child, who is the family leader and legislator. In our culture, with its relative emancipation of the female, the woman's social place is almost invariably dependent on the position and achievements of a man, her father or her husband, and her life is more segregated than his.

The ascetic ideals, mainly masculine in genesis, helped place woman in her deplorable social position. Because sexual desire is the most distracting "carnal lust" for him who wants to shield himself from the gross realities of existence and contemplate heaven, the ascetic and religious leader blamed the woman for those feelings of his own which she evoked. The early ascetics and through them the people to whom they gave their ideas denounced woman as vile, a vessel of iniquity, the instrument of the downfall of Adam. In churchly conclaves the divines questioned her possession of a soul and very definitely and legally denied her the right to the possession of property and her own children — *ad infinitum, ad nauseam.*

To protect herself and fulfill her needs in this man's world, woman has been forced to utilize whatever weapons fall to her, and the first of these, contradictory as it may seem, is her physical and social inferiority. Since people can gain their ends by various social devices, the display of weakness, which I call "the will to power through weakness," is used by the weaker in any social relationship. In this case, woman's tears and complaints have helped her establish her own brand of tyranny.

The second important weapon in her arsenal is her sex, because the man is the one to be aroused and to be put into an active state toward the woman. Declared seductive, she emphasizes seductiveness, and her life diverges from mere humanness into somewhat distorted sexuality. This adds to the color of life, gives it charm, keeps the sexual pot aboiling, but produces a hypertrophy of certain qualities and an atrophy of others.

When weakness and flirtatiousness are necessary for achievement or for success, then weakness and flirtatiousness are used. When strength and candor, honesty of purpose and activity are successful weapons, they are used.

Among the birds and mammals, the male is the more highly decorated and flaunts the sexual symbols. He grows the gorgeous feathers and the more luxuriant mane. His colors are the more vivid, and he exhibits himself in all his glory to win the female. In humans the reverse has taken place, and woman must bear a heavy burden in the struggle to be beautiful — a struggle, alas, destined for defeat even though there may be a brief victory. To be beautiful is possible only to a few and then for only a short period of life.

Superiority or inferiority, so far as most women are concerned, is curiously and deplorably artificial. An accidental, more or less useless assemblage of features can bring one woman into the limelight and make her the adored and emulated of thousands. Features just as good biologically proclaim a girl or a woman as ugly. A large nose is as good as a small one for inhaling air, but one extra quarter of an inch may create a state of mind good for the plastic surgeon though deplorable for the sufferer. The truly valuable human traits are put into a secondary category of esteem by artificial standards which shift from generation to generation, from place to place, and from social group to social group. The quest for beauty mars the character of the girl and woman: her energies are directed away from achievement and hardihood, and her egoism rests on a false basis.

Woman's use of her weakness, her sexual charms, and her beauty may be — and usually is — privately rewarded. It is also publicly damned. For thousands of years, woman's frailties have served as one of the favorite subjects of the authorities, who almost always are men. Ever since the man said: "The woman whom thou gavest to be with me, she gave me of the tree, and I did eat," man has been using woman as a scapegoat.

The scapegoat is the blame object, and from the two-year-old who kicks the threshold over which he has stumbled to the learned scientist who blames Mom for the neuroses, psychoses, and general maladjustment of poor Homo, there is an identity of primitive thinking and explosive emotion which leads to the selection of "whom to blame."

"But the goat on which the lot fell to be the scapegoat shall be presented alive before the Lord to make an atonement with him and to let him go for a scapegoat into the wilderness." Since that time scapegoats have been officially and unofficially selected to bear the brunt of the sins of the congregation. When Rome burned, the early Christians were sacrificed by the thousands to appease the wrath of gods annoyed by their obstinate wickedness. The persecution of the Jews, those eternal aliens, has always been justified by blaming them for the evils of capitalism, the rise of Communism, the tyranny of religion, the threat of antireligion, and all the contradictory phases of our complicated social structure.

The scapegoat, usually the other sex, race, group, or

fellow, is the constant victim of the frustrated and sullen mind — that is, the more or less chronic state of the mind of man. It takes a largeness of view and an unusual fairness of concept to divorce oneself from this tendency. The stranger, the alien in our midst, is always the convenient scapegoat, and if there is no stranger, some member of the group has to take on that function.

Woman has been one of the chief scapegoats, though she has not ordinarily been driven into the wilderness, since men, by a trite and true statement, are unable to live without her though, judging by the divorce rate, living with her seems increasingly difficult. The marriage ceremony is a gross deception when it proclaims that a man and a woman have been made one by it. They have been united and certain interests have been merged, but Oneness, never! Though women are the mothers, sisters, sweethearts, and wives of men, they are, in no small part, alien to them and generally not understood. Therefore all of the dominant religions have established woman, as Eve or Pandora, as the source of the evils that befell mankind, and the cause of his expulsion from a paradise in which he never dwelt.

The selection of the scapegoat is the easiest way to find a cause for the effect one hates, and so, as our most fashionable scapegoat of the moment, we have Mom, the cause of all neurosis. Thus some mothers overprotect their children; some of those children become neurotic; therefore mothers' overprotection causes neuroses! The reasoning is no more profound than that and is a good example of the fallacy of the positive instance. It has not the slightest basis in scientific proof since it neglects the cases where the overprotected do not develop neuroses, those in which the underprotected and normally protected develop neuroses; and it ignores all the other economic, social, and religious factors that work inexorably on any individual mother and her child.

Without the slightest statistical or even logical proof, with the twin fallacies of false selection and positive instance, one writer "proves" that all the soldiers who broke down in World War II did so because they were "their mothers' sons" and could not free themselves from mother love. Another writer declaims that all the revolutionaries, such as Karl Marx, who aspired to break down the entirely good social schemes of their day did so because of mother-fixation. Reformers are such, so the book states, because reformers are haters, not because there is something to hate and some evils to combat; haters are such because of their miserable childhood; and the blame for frustrated childhood can be placed upon the misdirected mother. Here, he writes, are the real causes of the French Revolution, Communism, woman suffrage, and so on. Every link of the chains of thought and reasoning in this book is partial and therefore misleading; it has not yet become good mathematics that ten times nothing is something.

Recently Mom has become known as a member of "the lost sex." If "lost sex" is broken down into items like crime, alcohol-addiction, neurosis, psychosis, and suicide, then the argument completely collapses, since crime is many times more prevalent in the male population, alcoholism is at least five times as frequent, the neuroses and psychoses taken all together are equally distributed, and suicide is three to four times more frequently a despairing act of men than of women.

Mom, poor Mom! I put on my shining armor of skepticism and rise to defend her. The authorities who attack her would do better to attack the other authorities who have guided and misguided her. The poor woman, like all human beings, seeks certainty and thus relies on authority, but has been barraged by all kinds of contradictory advice about child-rearing.

The authorities in this field swing like pendulums from one extreme to the other. Only a few years ago they told us not to pet children, call them endearing names, or show any outward affection toward them. Today they warn of affection-hunger and say that if children feel they are not wanted or loved, Heaven knows what will happen when they are grown. Just as authoritatively as they once enjoined the mother at the peril of her soul to feed the child every four hours (or whatever it was), now in the same portentous manner comes forth: "Feed him whenever he cries, so that he will not build up feelings of hostility and not-wantedness sooner or later to erupt as a neurosis or psychosis." Not long ago they said: "Spare the rod and spoil the child still holds good," that trees and children must be pruned. Yet today they decree that children must be allowed to do whatever they please and must not be inhibited or frustrated. As for diet, with the discovery of the vitamins and the advent of scientific nutrition, the authorities stated that no child could grow up healthy without spinach, orange juice, and pasteurized milk. I have seen children who grew up on the fruitless plains and steppes of Russia, in cowless China, in the shut-in little districts of France where red wine was given to them from childhood, who somehow evolved into solid, powerful, attractive manhood and womanhood. Yet in this country countless mothers, poorly advised, completely ruined their children's appetites by forcing them to eat certain foods in specific quantities. And now numerous experiments have been made which show that the child flourishes if allowed to follow, in some measure, his own desires in eating.

Dear reader, gentle and misguided soul, this is merely the eternal polarity of ignorance, the so-called swing of the pendulum. The ancient Jewish scholars had a name for it; they called it *"Tamar verkehrt,"* which means that turning things upside down may bring as satisfactory results in the seeking of truth as logic itself.

Many years ago I discovered that there can be no simple formula for raising children. When I was a young psychiatrist, father of one child, I loftily developed a lecture entitled, no less: "A Decalogue for Parents." Like a new Moses I enunciated ten commandments based on the successful rearing of son number one. Along came son number two, a nonconformist, who shattered my feelings of certainty. I changed the title of the lecture to "Ten Hints for Parents." With this modification of authoritarianism, I got along well enough until the third child was born, a girl; then I gave up the lecture entirely.

The complex matter of how we shall bring up our young in a complicated civilization should be based on a scientific collection of data, and this has not, as yet, in the least degree been approached in scope and adequacy, and probably will not be for a generation to come. The authorities who accuse poor Mom feel no need of scientific data, control studies, and experimental knowledge, but confidently spin dogmas from their heads and set forth, as from a new Mount Sinai, rapidly altering decalogues for parents.

Because of the insistence of the authorities, we see parents who blame themselves or are blamed by others for the neuroses of their children. Probably the most exaggerated of all modern statements about children and parents is that the parents reap what they sow by bringing up the child incorrectly. No one blames a parent if a child is born feebleminded, or color-blind, with clubfeet, or with six fingers and toes instead of the conventional five, "because" the great assembly line of human reproduction and production went askew with that child. It is perfectly well established that anything that changes the "timing" of the uterine development may produce inborn physical deformity.

Some traits of mind and personality are also congenital, inborn, and not made. You cannot make Einsteins to order, nor create by any special manipulation Shakespeares, Newtons, Goethes, Michelangelos, Picassos, or any type or kind of genius. Neither does environment account for the little Jesse Pomeroys who begin life with no capacity for moral development and become fiends at five, nor does it explain good families producing black sheep, who from the start are rebellious and stubborn and finally find a social level natural to the deprived and socially unfortunate groups, but utterly unnatural to them. It does not account for the child who shows terrific fear and anxiety long before he has had any experiences to account for his panic, and who remains unsocial from start to finish, perhaps developing schizophrenia as the natural goal.

Environment and the parents' guidance do not explain the out-and-out homosexual, who has no desire whatever for the opposite sex, but from the age of five on shows real lust for his or her own sex. In every department of natural drive, desire, instinct, development of social feeling and codes, development of artistic, literary, and scientific capacity, just as in every avenue of physical growth and development, there are mishaps, deformities, disproportions, absences, which are inborn, even though the environment may be favorable, unfavorable, or indifferent to that mental trait. The experiencer is as important as the experience — I think more so — in many of the interactions of potentiality and realization.

Whatever the cause, your little bad actor keeps his mother awake nights, enslaves her, and deeply injures her natural egoistic desire to rejoice and take pride in her child. Either he drives her into so deep a neurotic fixation on him that the normal children and husband are neglected; or he brings into her mind a hate for him, which must, she feels, be disguised and which horrifies her by its sudden explosions into her consciousness. For one mother who seems to drive a child into neurosis, there are many children who bring mental disorganization, deep suffering, and pointless living into the life of the parent.

Even without inborn deviation from normality, it must never be forgotten that psychologically the child is more a product of his times and special social influences than of his parents. How many kindly German parents were horrified by the savage teaching that their children got in the Nazi schools! The economic state of the parents and the community, the accessibility of education, the nature of the accepted religion and its peculiar hold on each individual, the kind of laws by which people live and their own status in regard to those laws (for example, above or beneath them), the currents and waves of emotion, mood, and experience — all these and many more things tend to make of the individual a somewhat individualized replica of the several types his culture builds.

I know many families where the importance of the children has been paramount, where whatever was done had them finally in mind, and where there was no dominance and no punishment. I believe these children would have benefited more from freedom increasing as they developed and especially as they earned it. It is my belief that at first the parent should be the benevolent absolute ruler of the state, since the infant has no judgment or knowledge. At two or three, perhaps at four, a constitutional monarchy ought to be set up with rules and rights for both sides, but with the power still in the hands of the parent. At puberty the parents become heads of a republic, since in height, strength, beauty, and intelligence — in fact, in all save experience — they are rapidly reaching second place. And sooner or later parents and children alike become fellow citizens. Happy is the home where this transition of status takes place gracefully, happy the home where the ever changing theories of publicity-seeking authorities on child development are excluded in the name of science and sense!

I am not writing a brief for the follies of mothers, since in my daily work I am, alas, too often appalled by the stupidities and cruelties of mothers, fathers, brothers, sisters, husbands, and wives and, in fact, of all groups and classes of human beings. It is a very tangled web, this civilization of ours, and we are all the victims of the follies of our ancestors, and, in some part, the authors of the sorrows of our descendants. We live under the pressure of institutions we did not create; we are obsessed by taboos and prejudices we have inherited almost as inexorably as we have inherited our skins. Mom thus is a victim of social pressure and its distortion, and this social pressure is mainly the creation of a long, confused, and complicating line of directives issued by the male commanders.

We have a long way to go in scientific understanding before we can find a real scapegoat for the maladjustments of human beings. We are our mothers' sons and daughters, likewise our fathers', but we are also the mental sons and daughters of all the institutions and of all the conflicting pressures of our confused and tensely disharmonious times.

There is a social psychopathology as real as individual psychopathy. To pick out Mom as the focus of that psychopathology is a gross injustice and, I say without any hesitation, utterly unscientific. In fact, it flouts the very essence of true science, which knows no scapegoats. With all her faults, which are as real as those of her mate, the female of our species is responsible for that tenderness which we call love. Not the fierceness of sexual passion, which is a primitive hunger and more apt to be cruel than tender, but the warm glow of gentleness and devotion. Without tenderness men would be cruel beasts with nothing at all to redeem them, and this world, bad as it is, would be infinitely worse and utterly hopeless. Perhaps here and there in its excess or misdirection mother love creates neurosis and maladjustment. *Perhaps* only, since we are far from knowing the cause of most of the mental diseases. Even if these accusations and denouncements have some slight basis in fact, Mom, Ma, or Mother, as you choose to call her, is a solid base of decent human social development. Without her there would be no home where the future authority could grow up and develop those qualities which he later uses partly for the good of man. In fact, without her there wouldn't even be a future authority at all!

CHAPTER VI

SOCIAL AMBIVALENCE

A SOCIAL worker once brought to the clinic where I was in charge a husky seventeen-year-old girl, pregnant but unmarried. Miss Seventeen-year-old had a pretty, feminine face and a strong, attractive female body. Few men would pass her by without a second look. She was vigorous and had gone along like a healthy female in the tremendous but entirely commonplace role she was playing in reproduction. She was neither feebleminded nor insane. The society in which she lived said unequivocally, and properly, that unmarried girls of seventeen must not become mothers. Because the girl had not adjusted to the laws of that society, the social worker wanted to know whether the girl was abnormal and whether she needed psychiatric care.

The girl, however, was not a psychopath. Age-old processes designed to bring about pregnancy in women had operated inexorably in her. Pituitary had spoken to thyroid and to ovary. Ovary had said: "Oh yes," and prepared breasts and uterus for pregnancy. In fact, ever since she was eleven years old, her body had been busy in every proper way preparing to receive a sperm. Part of the preparation was attracting and responding to young men. Her hormones sent out an urgent message; the opportunity presented itself in the shape of a desired man;

the oestrous cycle found its natural result in pregnancy. Biologically there was nothing to quarrel with in the sequence of events. Socially there was a quarrel and a serious one. She had disorganized the social structure. She was bringing a baby into a world not ready to receive him. She was entering motherhood without the basic essential, the protection of a mate, and her baby would be born at a great disadvantage. There was a time when she would have been jailed because of this unauthorized pregnancy, or she would have been scourged with a whip, and society's scorn and rage would not have started with a psychiatric examination. But mental disease had taken the place of sin as an explanation for this biologically necessary, socially condemned act. In a sense, this transition of attitude lost nothing of ominous import, for it is more deeply divergent to be mentally sick than it is to be sinful.

The social worker, on the other hand, was socially adapted, biologically completely maladapted. She was about forty years of age, sturdy, well built, albeit a very plain person, who made no attempt to be decorative. Her menstrual cycles had come and gone some four hundred times; her organism, made and oriented for pregnancy, had called out that number of times in vain. The lady was respectable and respected; she was intelligent, socially adequate, and indeed a very pleasant person. She never dreamed of asking whether she was a psychiatric case. But in a society organized on biological levels, she, and not the girl, would have been the misfit.

We can say, of course, that the social worker is like the worker in some insect aggregations and so is per-

fectly moral and normal in remaining virginal, in denying her biological drives. But in an insect organization
there is division of labor *with* physical organization. The
insect worker is neuter gender in bodily structure and
need not struggle with sexual instinct or drive. Some of
my patients have asked: " Why was I made this way if I
was to remain a celibate?" or, to put it more crudely:
"Why has an erect penis no conscience if society is
right?" Our social worker (or teacher or factory worker
or nun) is not a neuter; she is a woman with tears of
frustration and long, agonizing struggles, and sometimes
that worst of feelings, "What a fool I am!"

It was a social worker who told me the story of a man
visiting heaven. There he saw three women walking in
circles. After every few steps each woman administered
to her own buttocks a sharp kick. The astonished visitor
asked: "How long have they been doing that?" St. Peter
answered: "A century or more." "But why?" queried the
persistent man. "Well," said Peter, stopping to light up
his pipe, "when they got here, I asked their qualifications
for heaven. Each one promptly said: 'I have remained a
virgin.' Then to each I replied: 'That is of no conse-
quence here.' They have been kicking themselves ever
since."

Let us consider Kant's criterion of right and wrong, to
wit, what would happen if the deed or its omission were
universally applied. If the social worker's conduct became universal, there would be no problem at all, since
mankind's suicide would leave some insect free to rule. If
the unmarried mother's example were followed, there
would finally result chaos, since with no self-government

all social government would go. Nevertheless, if the goal of mere survival is the only solid purpose of what we anthropomorphize as nature, then the purely biologically normal is to be preferred over the purely socially normal, and the pathological person is the social worker and not her client. Certainly *to me* hormones seem more valid as a background for normality and even morality than St. Paul or his predecessors in Hebrew, Egyptian, or Indian morality.

I have used "biological" and "social" and the related nouns as if they were opposites or, at least, markedly different. Broadly speaking, biology includes sociology, since it is a prime biologic characteristic of man to be social. It is biologic for men to use tools, and therefore all mechanical development and the artificialities of the machine age are as much a part of the biology of man as his glands; it is biologic for *Homo sapiens* to think, and therefore all the seemingly fantastic restrictions and inhibitions he has placed on his more primitive urges are as biologic as the forebrain, which does his thinking. There are men who preach with passion against the use of medicines as nonnatural, yet they shave, wear clothes, brush their teeth, and use eyeglasses, to itemize a few of a thousand departures from nature, whatever that may be. I use the term "biological" to mean the expression of primitive bodily activities and needs, and the term "social" to denote those processes and demands which are represented by man's institutions and often show the dominance of tradition, custom, and taboo. There are psychologists who question whether man really has social instincts, yet the psychologists are men who live in groups and who could not survive or remain sane without sociality. There is no real dichotomy of biologic and social.

With no solution for this apparent disharmony, I still deny the validity of a scheme which balks and declares obscene man's fiercest cravings, those which build up the continuity of life. There is something wretchedly wrong in the whole ideal of chastity; it is something of an incubus on human life. St. Paul's contemptuous saying that it is better to marry than to burn has been amplified into a whole code of life which relegates sex, its pleasures, and its results to the position of necessary evils.

I am not wise enough to know how we shall establish a valid social physiology and social psychology of morality. Not, I am sure, on the authoritative thunderings of men who did not know about the ovum, the sperm, or the hormones; or of men who thought that plagues, floods, failure of crops, mental disease, and death came because God was displeased by some failure to observe rites. We would not run railroads by the notions of people who knew only about ox-carts.

It is important to realize that our ideas of sex date back to nomads who did not even know the paternity of the male, and who linked sexual happenings into a system of cause and effect with the great phenomena of nature. Drought, which was one of the dreaded events, was the effect of sexual sin, and adultery "caused" pestilence and cosmic punishment at a time when the stars, the planets, the sun and moon were believed to be concerned with the acts of the individual human being. For abundant confirmation of these beliefs, read the prophets, the Greek tragedies, and such anthropologists as Frazer. People lived and died in conformity with notions based not on facts but on magic and superstition. For these reasons, as well as the necessities of the group, came the regulatory forces directed toward the discipline and control of the sexual urges and acts.

In the course of time man, the incorrigible ceremonializer, artist, and meddler with his own functions and organs, reached the point, let us say, of our civilization. He declared sex to be sinful unless sanctified in certain ways. He declared obscene the parts essential to life and reproduction and decreed that they be hidden. At various periods he considered legs, bosoms, and even faces the instruments of damnation and decreed that they be covered since they stirred sexual feeling and thought. At other stages of his fantastic history, he slipped to the opposite pole of conduct and even offered his foreskin as a holy sacrifice to his God. He declared that if a man and woman became united by law and religion, they must entirely cleave to one another though everything between them might alter, though love might disappear, and hate, indifference, and contempt take its place. No other person might either permanently or temporarily engage the primitive and quite vagrant sexual desire.

But why go on? The regulations are absurd, but regulation has to be, since the animal in us is incapable of building up a society in which there is order, co-ordination, and stability. So we pass from the nonrational of the instinct to the "absurd" sanctions of society. Adultery does not concern God, nor are plagues the result of moral misconduct, but how else could the leaders of men, knowing nothing themselves, hold other men in check except through sanctions beyond reason? The social instincts or purposes of the individual himself — whatever term one wishes to use — demand the conformity of the sexual conduct to the approved pattern of the group, and the conscience of the individual becomes an ally of the social structure or society. The chief struggle comes within the scope of marriage, and the sexual problems of the mates find their way into the courtroom, express themselves in the rate of divorce or separation, as well as in neuroses and the alcoholic habit. The monogamous marriage has to compete with the various other forms of sexual life that are present in every community and represent the ambivalent attitude of society toward sex.

Since no legislation, no teaching, no preaching can really abolish the hormones, there develops an underworld of desire, a concealed world, a seething inner hidden life, which may or may not reach out for satisfaction. A recent book by Dr. Alfred C. Kinsey, widely read as a new and scientific form of pornography, shows what happens in this concealed inner world, although we psychiatrists have known about all this for a long time. Whether or not this underworld is unconscious is another question, although I think not. I believe it is merely hidden or disguised, an area of greater or lesser reticence *at times*, but not unconscious. By the right rapport and the right questions, the nice little woman seated before me will tell a tale of sexual fantasies and longings and of sexual conduct that her spiritual leader (if she has one) never hears and which she relates with downcast eyes at first, but with surprising candor and some relish at the end. With an underworld of demand, the mutilated sexual desires create an underworld of supply. In competition with marriage we find both prostitution and unorganized, noncommercial love affairs. And we must not forget homosexuality, incidental as it is in our civilization, although elevated to a cult in classical Greece.

The battle between the forbidden and the desired creates tragedy when the struggle involves serious persons completely enmeshed in such terms as "sin," "duty," "chastity," "passion," and "love." Nothing is so pathetic, because it is so ridiculous, as the great and high tragedy of *Faust*, wherein murder, damnation, hell, choirs of angels, God, and the Devil become cosmically (and comically) involved in a sexual affair between a human male and female. So, too, Dante's concept of Paolo and Francesca floating through hell eternally united by the sword of the betrayed husband is utterly barbaric, even though the great poet clothed it in beautiful words. The drama of *The Scarlet Letter* of Hawthorne belongs in the same category of "much ado about what?" All the fuss made because two organs that belong together get together must make the Power that Is grin sardonically. Fortunately, most of the world is incapable of high tragedy, and, like all obstacles that vex human desires, the inhibitions have roused circumventing forces. Even those devices which have tried to lessen sexuality have really increased it. A large part of the world's literature is the smutty story in one form or another, or the humor that essentially debunks the whole business of sex. Except in a few very rigid groups and during a few periods of time, the lip homage to chastity and continence has been offset by droll stories, bawdy songs, and a complete though hidden defiance of the sexual code.

All that clothes have really achieved beyond warmth is to increase the mystery and allure of the bodies that are hidden. A leg covered by a silk stocking is much more attractive than a naked one; a bosom pushed into shape by a brassière is more alluring than the pendant reality; most males are better imagined than seen. The differences between the sexes become tragically and erotically accentuated by dress; the more those differences are hidden and made mysterious, the more obsessive they become. Inhibition of a natural appetite, but with every daily contact enhancing that appetite, is like having a hungry man walk among living garnished steaks which he desires and which also ardently desire him.

So great is man's ambivalence that just as he develops codes and morals, so he seems to be deliberately making it impossible for morality to exist. Though pleasure be damned and the flesh declared vile, the stage, advertising, and business in general take no stock in such notions. They go as far as they dare in saying that pleasure is grand and the flesh sweet if appropriately clothed night and day, in and out of bed, and even into old age. Although churches may thunder about the vanity of beauty, more men are interested in beautiful and enticing women than in holy and righteous ones. The way to a man's heart is still an ancient road, and not via the gastrointestinal tract. While the official leaders of men preach and teach antibiologically, there remain many worshippers

of the oldest nature gods. The resulting social ambivalence, social and individual hypocrisy (without any
moral under- or over-tones), add storms and confusion
to the lives of men.

Let us take another example of the conflict between
biological drive and social injunctions. I shall now become John Bunyan in reverse and present the case of
Mr. Carefree and Mr. Careful. Early in his career Mr.
Carefree felt the urge to be free, to enjoy the fine and
gorgeous present moment. He became a good hunter,
he swam well, every now and then he skipped school because the sun was bright and all the tissues of his body
yearned for a pleasant expedition with his gang. Therefore he was not a good scholar, and because he was not
a great athlete either, he obtained a mediocre job. He
married early because that seemed right and necessary
to him, and soon he was burdened with more children
than he could readily support. We have then Mr. Average Citizen, secretly baffled, envious of the successful,
with silent despair as his constant but almost never expressed frame of mind. He failed because he could not
choose easily between that fine present moment which
leads to mediocrity and low status, and the self-immola-
tion that leads to wealth, or power, or social prestige.

He had a classmate, Mr. Careful, who pushed aside
everything that tended to interfere with his distant goals.
Calculating the cost of everything he did, he rigidly excluded the present moment of pleasure. He sold lemon-
ade for odd pennies, but never neglected his studies. The
swimming-hole saw him not. He played no kissing games
and never sat in the moonlight with a girl to whom his

young heart and fancy gave incredible beauty and an infinity that linked itself with all of poetry and music. He would have laughed at all that as foolish vaporing. In college he somehow found the most lucrative ways of making money, and he also discovered the cheapest places to live. For him there was no dillydallying along the road of life, no idle nonpurposive moments, no light-hearted laughter, no dalliance with Venus. A very moral young man, his morality was negative, for he never lifted a hand to help a fellow, nor could he spare a dime for the beggar whom he despised. Of course he made money. He married late and was a great catch, though he never gave his wife much more than possessions. He had a mistress because he learned somehow that it was the thing to do, but, truth to tell, he never tasted or bestowed ecstasy, and his immorality was as acrid as his morality. In his late middle life he became a philanthropist. He took money from the fools and improvident, as he called them in a rare but exceedingly frank moment, and gave the collected aggregates, which in their hands would have been "wasted," to institutions for fools and improvidents. With all this, I cannot say that he had more illness or more neurosis than other people who lived more naturally and gave some leeway to their desires and passions.

Neither Mr. Carefree nor Mr. Careful steered a good course between the perils of biology and the dangers of society. Mr. Carefree, following his biological urges, reached social deterioration. Mr. Careful, overindulging the acquisitive trends that society overrewards, achieved social prestige, but sacrificed pleasure and spontaneity. Neither of them reached real satisfaction.

We psychiatrists are fond of a slogan: "adjust to reality." But whose reality must one adjust to? The reality
of Mr. Carefree was quite different from that of Mr.
Careful. The reality of the predatory and acquisitive is
different from that of the gentle and self-denying, that of
the monk is not that of the hedonist, nor does the devoted
wife of a philosopher agree with him as to the validity of
their respective realities. The eunuch who looks after a
harem has different realities from those of the inmates,
and it is assumed that he is incapable of at least one reality of his master. If a society is psychopathic, foolish,
or criminal, as all societies are to a degree, must one adjust to that psychopathy or foolishness or cruelty? Is a
society normal in which war is extolled and the warrior
is the greatest man? Is it normal for men to give up play
and exercise and the bright sunshine at ten, or eleven, or
fourteen so that "the country" (meaning a few men)
may grow rich and export the products of the labor of
these ten-, or eleven-, or fourteen-year-olds? Was it
normal to adjust to the Germany of Hitler, to become a
servant of the state, to lose personal worth, to believe
in oneself and one's kind as the only *Volk*, to "*heil*" Hitler all day long, and to crush everything individual and
original in oneself, except as it gave the state more
power? Undoubtedly the German psychiatrists, studying
the case of an energetic, rebellious personality who blew
up banks and became a leader of the underground, did
exactly as we do in similar situations — namely, labeled
him as a psychopath and found the roots of his conduct
in some psychological trauma of his youth. Is it normal
to adjust to the stupidities of Main Street, or to the

hidden notions of a provincialism which form the back-drop both for wholehearted lust and for fierce asceticism? In a world still ruled by the stored-up thoughts and ideals of the dead, there are a thousand "normalities" competing for each man's adherence and demanding from him endless adjustments.

If normal mental life means adjustment to a normal society, there is no such thing. What irks me is the smugness with which most psychiatrists and psychologists accept our society as normal. I have heard endless discussions of crime and never heard that society needs reforming from top to toe. Never in any learned meeting have I listened to a paper which stated that we need a new social physiology of morals, including the sexual code, even if such a physiology would be difficult to establish and would involve battle with entrenched antiquity. Psychiatrists have never been leaders for good working-conditions, reasonable pay, and a decent social-economic ethics. It is true that they have worked for reforms in criminal codes and in the care of the mentally sick, but not on the grounds that society may be creating criminality and mental disease. Perhaps I myself have been too busy as a narrow-minded specialist.

Society expects man to be a passive social animal who believes like the people of the Field in *Jurgen* that "to do what you have always done" and "what is expected of you" are the twin rules of life. This, of course, is not true. The wanton crucifixion of impulses, the unnecessary blocking and frustration of the drives and urges, are an evil that reflects itself in sophistication, ennui and boredom, dissatisfaction, melancholy, fatigue, anxiety, and neurosis. The emotions and the inner visceral drives of mankind are not always amenable and often resist, overtly or covertly, the admonitions to behave properly. A man may be finally disciplined out of emotional expression and become a stolid passive personality, or he may be conditioned into irritability, exploding with violence into emotional expression of an adverse and disorganizing type.

Government and discipline are absolutely essential, lest men be plunged into habits of sensuality and disorganized yielding to impulse. Without them there would be a minor war whenever two people met or attempted to live together. With them we have civilization, and I prefer civilization, with all its terrible cost, to raw animality. All the things I love — order, beauty, literature, art, music, and science — otherwise could not be. But a good bookkeeper stresses liabilities as well as assets, and the liabilities of civilizing the human being are very great indeed.

CHAPTER VII

THE LIABILITIES OF LANGUAGE

LONG before the time when Francis Bacon so pungently dwelt on the perils of words in his famous "Four Idols," men recognized that the coins of communication might become debased and lead to disastrous and counterfeit ends. In recent times the growth of a sharpened scientific attention to the ways and means of human relationships, with the feeling that a diagnostic hunt into every corner of human life was necessary to save mankind from its masochistic self, has led to the science of semantics. On the lunatic fringe of semantics are those who believe that if words were strictly controlled (an impossible condition) as to meaning and use, the world would be saved, there would be no wars, mental disease, or prejudices.

I shall not waste any time in outlining even briefly the service words have given to man. It is impossible to conceive of the human side of man's life without symbols fashioned by the respiratory air, and later by the cunning hand of man as pictures, writing, and printing. Without language in whatever form, man would have only the unconscious heredity of the animal to link him with his past, and he could not strive for future goals of distant grandeur.

The assets of words are our culture and our great men,

our triumphs of literature and science, our measurement of space and our budding conquest of disease, the beauty we are able to give each passing thought and function, and, perhaps, the longing for the infinite and divine! But as a practitioner whose most compelling contacts have been with the disasters of life, it is natural, though perhaps unfortunate, that the liabilities of living and so of speech have come most poignantly to my attention.

In the first place, words enable the dead to rule the living. While this has its value, it made it possible for the teachings of one man, Aristotle, to arrest the advance of knowledge; for centuries it gave authority to a spurious antique notion about the antipodes; it enabled people who lived two thousand years ago to govern the sexuality, the food customs, and social habits of modern society. People model themselves in the pattern of saints who probably never existed; ambition takes toll of those who live on the fallacious fare of Plutarch's legends; and the myth gets extraordinary life and beauty from words that falsify reality. Words make men endure present evils because they can pore over a book that tells them that "the meek shall inherit the earth." The meek do prematurely inherit the earth — six or more feet of it.

Then too, we think we can taste of experience far more widely with words than without them; in fact, we can create that which never existed. Mistaking such verbal experiences for real living, we splash in a shallow pool. When we speak of the glories and glamour of war, we pass over the harsh, horrible fact that men look very ugly when dead, that a bayonet or a sword rips guts in a way that does not beautify or exalt killer or killed.

To illustrate the difference between words and reality, I might tell the story of a fiery Communist, fiery in words at least, who talked of revolution and barricades and the uprising of the proletariat as if he were talking of a spectacle in an opera. I asked him: "Look, my bloodthirsty friend, did you ever see one dead man? Did you ever see a man killed by violence, his head smashed in, his brains oozing out, his eyes staring and mouth repulsively open? Did you ever see a dozen such dead — a hundred — ten thousand? Have you heard the groans and curses of the wounded, begging the relief of death?" Well, though he had not, he was not impressed by my eloquent dilatation of horrors.

One day I was called to his house. His little girl had been injured by an automobile; she was unconscious and covered with blood. Fortunately I was able to assure the distracted man that his adored daughter would do well and that he had nothing to fear. He looked at me long and curiously and said: "From this day on, I am no revolutionary. What you said to me lingered in my mind even though I rejected your words as those of a comfortable bourgeois. Then when I saw my daughter unconscious and bloody on a muddy street, I visualized revolution, not as an abstract term, but as daughters and sons lying in filth, dead and mutilated."

I believe therefore that Dante could not have felt the reality of the eternal and horrible hells that he portrayed; that he intoxicated himself with the smell and the sounds of words and never tried to imagine the stench and screams. Children say: "I'll kill you"; people say: "You're crazy," without meaning more than a vague symbolism. Not thinking about the conflagration of which their words are a distant glow, men can go on from one unfelt symbolism to another and finally reach a fanatic belief in something of which they have no concrete knowledge at all. I know ardent socialists who passionately love their private property and yet are able, by verbal magic, to live at once in two worlds, one of real capitalism and the other of verbal socialism. I know "free people" who talk glibly of homosexuality and adultery without ever translating the word into the deed, who thus "know the words, but not the music."

Words enable us to juggle with far more experience and ideas than we can digest, and they cover our real selves with a veneer that actually isolates us from real experience. To say more or less than one "means" is a chief social function of words. Then, too, words become magic and acquire mystic meanings which give a fictitious beauty to concepts actually repulsive and foolish. While this may have been the necessary way for men to travel to science and achievement, we can now throw these crutches away.

Men have died by the millions because of adjectives that became abstract nouns, so that a relatively good deed is Good, the disliked is Evil, and Sincerity and Faith are canonized even though there are sincere tigers and faithfull Hindu thugs. A book could be written about this transition of adjectives into nouns and thence into transcendental worshipful logic.

False unities are established, so there emerge the Jew, the Negro, the Protestant, the Catholic, This Country. Along with this slender-minded unification, its opposite, the disease of dichotomy, starts doing its deadly work. Thus, Body and Mind become separated, and the word "materialist" becomes a reproachful opposite to the word "idealist." So appear the absolute Good and Bad, God and the Devil, with concomitant splits like Pure and Impure, Holy and Unholy, Virtue and Sin. Words are necessary condensations and short cuts. Just as we cannot lug around a hundred pounds of bread to exchange for something else and therefore "buy" with the symbolic value of money, so we may use the word "mountain" to mean an endless rocky ecology. We must not, in the case of either money or words, forget in what the real meaning and values lie.

Especially in the field of the obscene and vulgar, words become more important than deeds. I remember a very up and coming young surgeon who said to me after reading *Lady Chatterley's Lover*: "What an obscene and horrible book!" "Why?" I inquired with malice aforethought. "Because of the obscene words of the lovers," he replied. "Well," I said, "you are thirty-two years of age, unmarried, and I suppose you are still a virgin?" He looked at me with unutterable scorn. "I am? Like hell I am." "Then," said I, "you think the word is worse than the deed."

When *Strange Interlude* was to be produced in Boston, the censor intervened and forbade its exhibition because it gave such a stark dramatization of sex. Yet the total effect of this grim tragedy was to *lessen* sexual desire rather than to heighten it. At the same time burlesque shows, which heightened the sexual impulses though they avoided the obscene and forbidden words, were permitted on several stages in Boston. In one the word was frank and so the play was forbidden. In the others the act was frank, but the word was not and so they were permitted.

I must tell of another case where words took on foolish and false values. A colleague and I were examining a poor Italian immigrant. My friend, a very fine Boston Brahmin, was asking the questions.

"Tony," he asked, "do your bowels move well?"

"Bowels, bowels," the patient repeated slowly, with wrinkled brows. "What means 'bowels'?"

A look of anguish came over the questioner's face. Then he brightened up. "Look, are you constipated? Do you have diarrhea?" he asked hopefully.

Tony's face dropped. "Constipa — I can no say it — what means it?"

My colleague turned to me and saw a broad grin on my face. He knew I had worked on the water-front of Boston, that I had lived in the slums, and that words were — just words to me.

"You ask him, Abe," he said.

"Tony," I asked, "do you shit all right?"

Tony's face lit up beatifically, for the light of a great understanding linked him with me. "Oh, shit," he said, "that my trouble — shit, shit, alla the time."

Now, my friend, who is Anglo-Saxon to the bone, can use the word "feces," the Latin equivalent, without a gulp, he can equivocate by "move the bowels," but he cannot use a good Anglo-Saxon word that happens to have become vulgar.

Once I carried out a critical experiment on a large

audience in the Community Church of Boston, an assemblage that may be classed as "liberal." Discussing obscenity, I said: "If I were to talk on the subject of sexual relationship and use the words 'organs of generation,' none of you would be at all disturbed. If now I turn Greek for the moment and say for the external organs of generation 'phallus' and 'lingam,' even those of you who know the meanings of these words will still sit quietly in your seats. But if now I turn Latin and so use the words 'penis' and 'vulva,' I see you squirming in your seats, some of you blushing, others with your heads down, and I hear a few titters — you are really uncomfortable. So I will turn English, say of the thirteenth century, and use the terms that nice people used in those days — good four-letter Anglo-Saxon words." I paused. "If I did, the police would arrest me and you would never forgive me. Yet these four-letter words, so redolent of obscenity and so devastating to your peace of mind, mean nothing more or less than the words you and the police permit me to use."

It was, I think, a sad day when certain words became harshly proscribed. At first this was merely the taboo of a magic-obsessed group and dates from such notions that the name of the Lord must not be taken in vain (indeed, 'his name is a secret). A fictitious trend was given to conduct. Caste and class entered into this discrimination, as Gurth eloquently states in an impassioned outburst in *Ivanhoe*. In fact, obscenity and the taboo of certain words is merely part of the caste stratification of society and should really be opposed by all believers in democracy. Society condemns as outcast the short and pungent four-letter words which like "rock," "punt," and "duck" are our best, because they are our shortest symbols.

While we use words to bite off far more than we can chew, let alone digest, and while we use words as if they in themselves are sacrosanct or outlawed, a more fundamental difficulty lies in our use of them as substitutes for red-blooded living. At any rate, the angry word becomes the necessary substitute for the blow of anger and hostility. Perhaps with great control we let our wrath, which could be discharged with just one buffet, simmer at the continued heat of pale sarcasm, or bitter sardonicism, or a nagging but ethical flow of soothing words. This is truly an impasse of our civilization. Compared with the hereditary gestures, the bared teeth of anger or the clutched hands of hate, words are incongruous and give little or no relief. Likewise, we may not shriek in fear, but must make some jesting remark or filter out the seething terror by a whispered dread. This is, of course, not the direct fault of language, but of a discipline made possible by words and words alone — always this incomplete reaction to the passions that rack our souls. By becoming articulate we have, it seems to me, become so straitened that there is little escape for what seethes within. I have long felt that what we most need in our harried lives are not sanatoria but *screamatoria*.

There is a substitutive life made possible by those derivatives of words, the book, the stage, and the screen. I am not one of those who speak with scorn of escape. There is, let us say, a threatening lion in my path, and if I can escape, why not? We put up screens to escape flies and mosquitoes as we put money in the bank to escape destitution. Escape, like all other constructive reactions, is necessary and natural to us, and I writhe when I hear it used as a term of reproach. But when we flee from our duties and obligations into a literary never-never world of sex without organs, love without fatigue and boredom, work without failure, and the heart's desire because of the head's emptiness — then we do escape fatuously and to the disintegration of our manhood and womanhood.

When we bury ourselves in a sentimental literature empty of the viscerality and imperfections of life, or a sensational literature of murder mysteries in which death has no meaning except to exercise the ingenuity of a detective, we escape from trouble and difficulty into idle fantasies. Our minds become progressively less able to face the real difficulties the more these foolish words in books or phantoms on the screen become ways of escape. I do not think, as some do, that this is the road to mental disease, but I do believe that such disuse of the mind brings loss of its qualities of strength, originality, and endurance and changes us into a vacuous folk fit for any foolishness, ready victims of the false authorities. Democracy in education is not impressive in its results, and he who worships the common man as if his commonness were a virtue is like a gardener who sows his garden with the poorer seeds. Justice to the common man, yes; opportunity for the common man, yes; but still the exceptional men will leaven the race.

Now I turn to the heart of the problem of words, the ambivalent result that is the glory and tragedy of man. All that has been said before in this chapter has been said many times and, I dare say, much more eloquently.

I now lay an emphasis on the power of words and a trend
of mankind which, so far as I know, has rarely been ex-
posited. There are several intricate processes that go on
together so tightly interwoven that only an artifact of
dissection can separate them. I shall merely describe the
process by which the naïve human being, whom we can
only postulate, becomes the seething, brooding creature
we know — or at least I know.

The codes of accepted conduct, different for each culture, group, and caste, gradually become imposed on the
raw human infant. At first nothing he does is wrong or
improper; in fact, we love his delicious animality and
complete lack of restraint. So great is our concealed and
inner rebellion against the very codes we carefully incul-
cate that one of the favorite sources of humor is the
enfant terrible who exposes the hypocrisy of his double-
talking elders. There is the famous story of the child who,
enjoined always to "do for others," asks: "What do the
others do?" Our delight in the child's exposed body and
mind eventually gives way to a gradually increased severity of teaching, a pressure mediated through words of
praise and blame. The eternal "Why?" of the three- to
four-year-old finally gives way to a crushed curiosity or
a disguised and hypocritical peering as the barraged elders ultimately take refuge in the most infamous subter-
fuge of all: "You must not ask about that." Long ago that
answer satisfied at least the parents, for then they took
literally the injunction that there were zones of "no tres-
passing" for the human mind. Today they are appalled
by their own hypocrisy.

To turn a child into a student; to postpone, or even

crush, his yearning for play, the natural avenue of learning and energy discharge; to make him wash his face, brush his teeth, be polite and refined, and continually curb the animal in him needs a constant admonition and the building up "within himself" of a censor, admonisher, hider, revealer — something to act in place of the accepted social authorities, but also something that seeks to fool those same authorities.

The child is not yet a separate personality until he can think of himself, not as James or Alice or what not, but as "I," which consciously separates him from the universe. At first he talks aloud and charms his elders by his running commentaries on what he is doing or about to do. Then suddenly, or perhaps gradually, he learns that he can talk to himself in a hidden way and people cannot know what he thinks! If he can make his words and his face behave as he wishes, he has an inner world. He now has a life of his own!

The great human development, the essential factor in conscience, arrives when he can say to himself: "You!" Thus begins something approaching the ambivalence of society itself, the inner struggle and inner debate, the most dangerous gift of the gods of language to man. The private world now becomes the introverted world. The inner debate between the various selves and hostile purposes assumes a role that in some remains minor and sporadic, but in others becomes never ending, and in many evolves into delusion and hallucination.

Whether the words that are used in this inner world are in part silently formed by the organs of speech, as some claim, or are motor images of sound quickened into life within the brain itself, does not matter to us. For myself, I must say this — that I think in words all day long and have visual images only when I am very tired or about to fall asleep. Then, to my delight, the inner dialogue almost ceases and I know sleep is around that magic corner whence the desired comes. I am not conscious of any motor equivalent to the "inner hearing." When I have something to write, I can often close my eyes and relax, and then a long lecture takes place without "I" or "you" to plague me. So I can be at perfect ease and there is no turmoil. But let a personal problem arise, let there come that eternal battle between the forbidden and the desired, let there be the realization that I have made a palpable mistake, let there arise the moral issue, and there is no rest, no relaxation, no long lecture, but instead the great debate, the Dialogue: "You — you — you — only a mistake — a little foolishness, you fool, you — you damned ass," and even harsher words, more damning phrases. Or, because we must not draw too one-sided a picture, complacency and self-approval also take the center of the inner stage: "You are pretty fine — not bad, not bad, old fellow. . . . Well, you carried that off with a swagger." There is, however, little turmoil with self-laudation and narcissism. Inner smugness rarely calls the "you" to the fore, but inner condemnation and struggle do. It is as if an inner Nathan the Wise confronted an inner David the King, and finally brought to him that most magnificent of climactic accusations: "Thou art the man!" In fact, to the learned in Biblical history, that simple declaration of guilt has become the essence of the inner reproach from which even tyrants are not exempt.

The inner dialogue records, explores, and shows new significance in the events of the past. Frequently the new meaning is fictitious. People now re-examine their childhood to find fixations and dominations, which are usually only the "new look" in psychologizing. Or those in the grip of melancholy find by retrospective analysis that some peccadillo was the mortal sin. Or, in seriocomic form, what she really meant those many years ago, when she said this or that, comes out in the light of experience as something one has missed. There are probably as many people who regret their lost opportunities for irregular diversion as those who become censorious critics of their past. Could we really reach into the concealed rumination of the elderly, we would find as many regretful saints as repentant sinners.

This shift to the past, which may chain a man to the futile, since the past lives only in its results, is not so anguishing to many of those whom I have known as their strange ability to swing into the future. I am quite sure no other animal regrets the past; I am as sure that to the most developed of our primate relatives the future is either the unconscious hereditary goal of an instinct or a dimly prefigured immediate sequence. I believe Pithecanthropus and even early Cro-Magnon with his "Ho-ha" and hisses and a few verbal nouns could not explore the world of his children's children, could not desire in "an infinite vestibule of denial" for the sake of a future world. He could not, I believe, foresee and torture himself with "social anxiety," the fear that in this or that important gathering or tête-à-tête "I shall grow pale, look like a fool, disgrace myself, pass wind, vomit, tremble, or be outshone by him or her to my own abasement." The great social law "Do what is expected of you" carries with it its pernicious polarity: "I may fail and do what is not expected of me."

So continuous dress rehearsal for the future event takes place within the troubled mind. "You do this and that, you are just as good as the other fellow, start off with some remark about how lovely she looks," and so on are the words that torture the socially uneasy. Only man foresees and fears the futures of sin, sickness, and death. Some men are endlessly preoccupied and tormented by a continuous verbalization of these themes.

The self-confident may also rehearse, but without great turmoil. Their inner discussions are about everyday events — the sea of social scrutiny in which we all live and to which we react with ease and grace, or with fear, or with some reaction in the complete spectrum between the two. In the hidden language of the turmoil within, we all discuss our struggles to be proper or admired, and debate social co-operation versus intense competitiveness.

This inner turmoil contains the murder that is never committed, the rape that stays within the head, the defiance of custom and authority which is stifled stillborn. Here rage disgust, exasperation, and despair, which come from the poisonous fatigue of never-ending duties and obligations. Here the drudge, doing the dirty work of life, seethes and boils behind a patient, dull exterior; here the mother, father, husband, wife, daughter, son, and what you will hide the disillusionments, destructive impulses and the "I wish I . . . you . . . he . . . she . . . they were dead" reactions. Here Hamlet solilo-

quizes: "To be or not to be," and Ecclesiastes finds its
grand pessimism. Here, unspoken, is Thoreau's "despair
of the average man," which now and then flames up into
private murder or public revolution.

All the eternal conflicts between duty and desire, obligation and freedom, crudity and refinement, the burden-
some and the sensual, the tyrannical future and the
planless present create this smoldering turmoil. All the
vagaries of desires and the vagrancies of dreams which
float into the mind of the most ordered life pop in and out
in the hidden words. I dare say that to make a twenty-
four-hour record of the flow of repressed but conscious
words of any normal inner life would outspan Joyce's
Ulysses by a dozen volumes and would seem an unbeliev-
able, unprintable schizoid nightmare.

Within this brooding inner world real murder, rape,
and rebellion are born, as well as the inhibited "inburst"
of baffled man. Here, also, genius incubates its eggs; here
are born in flashes and in long-planned wearisome effort
the greater or lesser creations of man; here the world is
taken apart and reborn as utopias of the past, present,
and future; here the word is carefully shaped into phrases
that move men into wildest fantasy and give the deepest
peace; and all that art, religion, philosophy, and science
have woven into life has its genesis in the hidden dialogue
and debate.

One can break up this hidden inner world into conscious, subconscious, unconscious; into id, ego, superego; into the vegetable, animal, and spiritual souls; but
these divisions are mere contrivances of men straining to
divide and unify, and also to be different and original. It

is to mistake the hidden and concealed as radically different from the exposed and revealed; it is to mistake a spectrum for black, white, and color.

This seething inner verbalization, whether it conceals or reveals the present urges and clamorous instincts, or burrows into the imagined or real fact, or projects itself into the desired or apprehended future, is not at any point to be separated from either the body or the social structure of man. In other words, its apparent pure "psychism" is also an illusion. The inner life of the old man is different from what it was when he was young, since the springs of feeling and drive have dried up, leaving, as the prevailing verbal streams, rumination and resignation for the wise man, and bitterness, melancholy, and fear for the defeated sick. When the seminal vesicles are tense, the sexual daydream predominates; when they are discharged of tension, the inner current takes a new direction. I am not implying that matters are as simple as these examples, but there is no moment when bodily tensions do not accompany our thoughts, and the more violent mental struggles inevitably involve the bodily functions.

It is difficult to say why this inner turmoil is excessively troubling only to some individuals. The shy and socially uneasy person is plagued by his inner turmoil "because" the scrutiny of others is painful to him, because he has not enough egoism, because he was dominated by his mother and rendered impotent, because his glands do not function well, because of inherited qualities or inherited lack of social power (why not?). The overscrupulous have a back-and-forth verbalization within them because religion over-inhibits, because they fear hell-fire, because they lack security (which brings to the fore a hundred becauses), and because their glands do not secrete enough this or that. Whatever the battle is about, it differs in degree, in constancy, in theme, in inner absorption and retreat from the outer world of action. It is conditioned by time and place, by whether the individual lives B.C. or A.D., during the Renaissance or the Victorian age, or after World War II; by whether he resides in Samoa, Palestine, Greece, Middletown, U.S.A., or some village in Australia. It is influenced by his status, by whether he be king, peasant, slave, rich or poor. It is modified by his personal attributes of beauty, strength, health, intelligence, emotionality, and endocrine balance. It is changed by countless environmental forces, which may be the book he has just read, the preacher he met, the alluring girl versus the kind of wife he has. It is the result of all of the shuffling, interweaving, integrating, and disintegrating factors of a life into which a universe of forces and events enters, per force, per chance, perhaps.

I have had as probably my main business in life the understanding of this inner turmoil. I have learned to disregard the material that is put forth as truth by the sick and the well, for I know that even with my status of trusted psychiatrist the words of the people I deal with are those which pass the social filter. The filtrate of speech that remains behind contains not only the forbidden, improper, indiscreet phases of reality, but also those memories, impulses, and reactions which cannot be summoned at will from the depths of experience and desire. There are accessible memories, relatively inaccessible memories, and the completely forgotten; I take no stock in the assertion that every experience is forever stored away in some magical filing system. It may either be woven completely into the individual's structure, and so lose its identity; or be so dynamically maintained as images and words that it can be readily recalled. I hardly need add that every controversy, every lawsuit, and countless experiments show how each individual selects and distorts the details of his experiences. Your child's mischief is to you adorable evidence of his vigor and vitality, to your neighbor proof that he is a loutish brat, without a vestige of charm. And so you both record it in your memories. The fact is that every experience is modified by the experiencer.

I have appreciated the complete concealment of the real inner life when I have seen professionally people whom I knew very well socially. Their disclosures left me marveling at the baffling intricacy of our social lives. It can happen, for instance, that the seemingly self-confident and gracious lady turns out to be a seething caldron of timidity, hatred, and self-derision.

Man's life took a perilous and glorious direction when he could speak to himself, when he could objectify himself as "you" and become the object of self-praise, self-hate, self-exhortation. It was then he learned to interweave past, present, and future into a bewildering kaleidoscopic pattern. It was then he discovered that sometimes the past is the only reality though it is actually long dead except for its effects; that sometimes the present is a macabre dance of masked unreal people, with outward decorum and conformity, and an inner seething underworld of primitive desires; and that always the future, which rises and falls with the crescendo and diminuendo of each moment's fantasy, offers torment or bliss unreal but more powerful than any reality.

CHAPTER VIII

THE ILLUSION OF INDIVIDUALITY

WHAT is the nature of individuality? Is its apparent emergence in me and you and all living things a reality or an illusion? Is it good or bad to try to be different, to seek the isolation of uniqueness; or are the followers of Buddha wise when they strive to lose their individuality and gain a mystic merging with the universe "as the dewdrop slips into the shining sea"? Can we label some of the great swings in human affairs as efforts for and against individuality? Democracy, let us say, emphasizes the essential basic worth of the individual, and totalitarianism fiercely denies that worth and sets up a sort of giant unit value, the state, into which individuality disappears. Is there here, as elsewhere in life, a necessary inconsistency so that one *lives* by a certain naïve postulate of individuality, although reason and science may deny the validity of that impelling belief?

It would seem certain that things, living or nonliving, are discrete, separate, and individual. I can look at you and see you as an object bounded by your skin, which even in the ecstatic embraces of love or the fierce struggles of clutched hate, separates you from beloved or enemy. Outer and inner seems to relate to that skin; microcosmos is within, macrocosmos is without.

The skin is a visible, tactile boundary, but it is also

the place of intense interaction between that thickened and visible node we call the individual and the environment of forces that flow in and out of him, making him up and breaking him down, acting in reciprocal relationship with him. Cut the skin of any individual and the blood that flows out is what Claude Bernard called the inner environment.

If you put coal in a stove, the coal does not become part of that stove, and while the heat engendered warms up the stove, the rise in temperature is no necessary part of the life of the stove. If the coal is environment to the stove, it remains so; it never penetrates the stove, nor does the stove ever enter into some reciprocal relationship with the place from which the coal came, so that neither can exist without the other. This differentiates stoves and all machines from the mechanisms called life.

Neglecting for the moment the apparent individuality of a living creature like man, let us make visible the invisible net of the universe in which the individual seems to have an autonomous and quite personal existence. In the first place, each of us comes from a unicellular egg, which was fertilized by another unicellular structure called the sperm. This minute organism carries all the hereditary potentialities around which our lives are built, not merely the potentialities of our immediate family or even our human ancestors, but even those which link us by unseen chains of descent and relationship to all the life of the world. Thus we have a unicellular heredity, which is part of the real life of each cell of our body. These cells live in our internal environment in a little salt ocean of their own, breathe oxygen, give off carbon dioxide, burn sugar, and manufacture ferments and catalysts, thus exhibiting the primary animal capacities of the living things that first populated the earth and are still its basic inhabitants. Consciousness? Awareness? Memory? Who knows? But the potentials of all these are in that fertilized ovum.

The unicellular ancestor, still present within us, develops into more complicated forms, with specialized and standardized functions, so that there appear on the scene orders and classes of living things, of which the main differentiating forms and functions are hereditary and are present within us. Thus we have a *vertebrate heredity* relating us to all creatures with backbone and a nervous system, with a spinal cord and a supreme collection of nerve cells called the brain. We have a *mammalian heredity* binding us to those creatures which develop their young within a uterus, nurse them at the mammæ or breasts, and have a tendency to care for their young and their mates. Then we have a primate heredity tying us to those other animals with a larger brain and more flexible limbs, which end in appendages like hands and feet. More differentiating links bind us to all types of Homo, to red, black, brown, or white Homo, to this or that type of red, black, brown, or white Homo, and thence to groups and families of Homo. Each phase in evolution is present within us by some unknown hereditary process which accounts for the great likeness of life.

United to every cell that has ever lived, we hang invisibly from a tree of life. Our likeness to other creatures is the greatest system of facts of our life; our differences are relatively minor. We are even in a firm reciprocal relationship with all plants. Since their expired gas is in our inspired oxygen, and our expired carbon dioxide is their inspired gas, we and they breathe reciprocally. Though seemingly separate from us, they are part of a system of which we are a different collaborating part, just as there might be two co-ordinating buildings to a power plant.

The reciprocity of food intake is just as dramatic as that of breathing, though much of it takes the grim form of the agent called Death. Practically all animals are incapable of building up carbohydrates; but the green leaves of plants perform this feat of magic by uniting carbon dioxide from the air with water from their roots and, with the co-operation of rays from the sun, finally evolving the carbohydrates needed by animals. For this process to be accomplished, the soil must be prepared both by earthworms and by certain bacteria that work on the dead bodies, the feces, and urine of animals in the earth so that plants can use them.

When the animal eats the plant, digests it, and absorbs part of it into his bloodstream, the products of the activity of the plant are brought to every cell of the animal. The cell is very small compared with the human being; it is very large compared with the molecules of amino acids, sugar, and oxygen with which it deals; in fact, it is like a good-sized factory compared with the material it uses. Whatever action takes place as a result, part of the material is built up into the body of the cell; *the plant literally becomes the animal.* Part of the material is burned, but with far less heat than any furnace could generate, and energy is set free for the functions of the animal.

Then comes a swing back to the environment. The cell returns the used material to the bloodstream, and thence it goes to the lungs, the kidneys, the sweat glands, and the bowels. These four avenues of excretion are certainly for the benefit of the individual. His respiratory tract rids him of a poisonous gas; his urinary system keeps him cool and non-toxic; his sweat excretion helps to maintain a constant inner temperature; and his bowels move out the waste products to rid him of superfluous material and make room for new food. This benefit to the individual, while important enough, is no more important than the good he does to other living structures. The carbon dioxide he exhales, the burnt-up cellular products he excretes through kidneys and bowels, are all necessary to the nutrition of the plant.

"Back to the plant" may take a short time or millions of years, since it may be hindered by man. It is not a conscious aim or purpose, but consciousness, the essence of the feeling of individuality, is necessarily separate from the purpose of this reciprocity. At any rate, the collection of tubes and cells we call a human being is a two-way system, to and from the environment; and to call his skin his real boundary is to eliminate sunlight and plant and soil and a thousand ingoing and outgoing streams and cycles of materials and energy.

Man, as I said, is a collection of tubes and cells. It is interesting to note how the "tube" motif has been played up by nature. The transition from the hole to the tube is logical and inevitable. No matter how closely knit a thing is, the microscope reveals that it is full of holes. In the course of evolution the primitive cell develops special tubes where separate and complicated functions and relationships are worked out. When the animal eats his food, he takes it into a complex tube called the gastrointestinal tract, really a turned-in part of the external environment, which is lined by digesting factories in the walls of the mouth, esophagus, stomach, and bowels. With the aid of innumerable bacteria, the food is prepared for absorption. When the food leaves this turned-in external environment, it passes into another series of tubes, the blood vessels, as part of the bloodstream. So the modified plant, the external environment, now becomes the *internal environment.* After the food is utilized, the end products are carried back to the outside world through the tubes of the respiratory system, the tubes of the kidneys, the sweat tubes, and the tubes of the bowels.

It would be difficult to depict the multitudinous ways in which the world streams in and out of the physiological chemical life of man; such an exposition would mark the progress of biological science. The history of scientific adventure in this field is studded with the names of great men who broke down the dogmas built by theologians, philosophers, and medical men. Physiologic research has broken away from theologians almost completely; philosophers only dillydally with the theme nowadays; and while doctors of medicine still rule the roost as the authorities on man, the time is clearly at hand when biologists, physicists, chemists, and, let us hope, ecologists will furnish the facts and the larger theories by which physiologic science advances. A Harvey could discover the circulation of the blood just by studying any man during life and after death, but to discover the nature of the food cycles takes biologists, botanists, chemists, physicists, ecologists, and doctors of medicine, as well as mechanics and technicians of all sorts.

What is responsible for the illusion of individuality? The human individual maintains his relationship with the external world by a two-way system of communication, the sensory nerves, which bring stimuli from the environment to the central station, where experiences are recorded and organized, and the motor nerves, which then carry back the impulses for whatever external motion is necessary. These physical processes are mysteriously linked with sensation, meaning, and memory, mental processes that are the building stones of the feeling of subjectivity, of each man's illusion that he is a self-limited microcosmos. Only with the development of consciousness comes each individual's conviction that he is a separate entity, discrete from his environment.

The part of the body that is the most individual and at the same time the most closely connected with the environment is the face. Here are located the great receptors for the physical stimuli of light, sound, odor, and taste. The eyes, the ears, the nose, and the mouth are the great channels by which the environment streams in as events called psychological, just as the mouth and nose are the portals for basic environmental relationships called physical.

Probably because the face is the most differentiated part of the human anatomy, it is the chief locus of self-feeling. In a thoroughly artificial way it has become the criterion of beauty, desirability, worship, or hatred and almost more important than the sex organs themselves in certain secondary phases of passion and love. The difference between the face that launched a thousand ships and one that would not launch a toy boat may be merely an eighth of an inch of nose, somewhat different eye pigment, and more or less yellowness to the hair. A straight line is more beautiful than a curved one only in the case of the nose. All these criteria of beauty are mere artifacts of racial self-worship and bigotry. It is utterly false that eyes widely separated indicate good character, that round red lips mark the passionate woman. Evaluation of self and others by "face value" is perhaps the most stupid and one of the cruelest of social attitudes of a world in which stupidity and cruelty are the rule rather than the exception. The non-seductive face may be far better functionally. A good face is merely one with a nose large enough and wide enough for a good current of inspired and expired gas, eyes neither near- nor far-sighted, an adequate oral cavity enclosing healthy teeth, and all this surmounted by a cranium large enough to hold a good brain.

Personality does not seem to relate equally in the parts of the human form: it seems to be centered in the face, where the give-and-take with the environment is at its greatest. Our life with others is carried on mainly by our facial social interchange. Our speech is our chief form of communication, deception, co-operation, and competition; our eyes are the center of I-ness and You-ness; and our revealment and concealment of emotion are most intimately and most discernibly expressed in flush, blush, and pallor of skin and all our varied facial expressions of joy, hatred, defiance, love, elation, or despair.

Much of our feeling of individuality comes from the institution of the home. Originally man was probably a herd animal, living in a large group. Then came the house and the home, the isolation mechanisms of civilization. Their doors and locks symbolize the actuality of the situation: that here a little group lives secure from intrusion, barricaded against indiscriminate social influences. These barricades are present as caste levels, as rejection of some social attitudes and acceptance of others. They build up a prop of pride in the smallest of the units of society, the family itself. For most people the family is more important than the group. The home and, quite curiously, the male family name give a spurious individuality to many human beings brought up in the modern patriarchal system. They cannot realize their unity with others, nor get the full impact of social circumstances, and often they become maimed in their capacity to be at ease with their fellow men. Within the home the individual seeks that rest, ease, security which in some fortunate instances he obtains, although in many cases the family is the center of an intimate and continuous storm of tension and disastrous ambivalence of emotion and purpose.

But with the development of a greater individuality, sociality becomes more difficult. Most people pass from the isolation of the home into the larger social life either with ease or at least with moderate facility. Still others have so great a bias away from sociality that they are deeply self-conscious, find it difficult to mingle with people, and even feel endangered by living and working outside the home. For them the home is the selfish center, or the peace center, or the security center of their lives, and obsessively so. For them the home is a barrier to objective living and heightens that subjectivity which, in its excess, is a grim peril to mental health and the joy of life.

"Art for art's sake," "Science for science's sake," are slogans for lofty intellectuals. But can even the artist or the scientist live in an isolated, vacuolated tower cut off from the currents and purposes of human existence?

It is somewhat arrogantly stated that the artist need have no purpose other than pure color, pure design, or pure form, with technique the all-in-all, and meaning nothing. Actually, there is no possibility for such an independence of art. By the time the man reaches the maturity of development whereat he can become an artist, he has already been immersed in society and his purposes are already social. Even if they are declaredly antisocial, they correspond to the statement of the group to which he belongs or which he hopes to lead. He has revolted from purpose because that has been emphasized too much for his taste, and his very revulsion is socially conditioned. No man can draw an impenetrable mantle around himself and say: "I am an individual." There can be no art for art's sake any more than there can be an artist who lives outside of the co-operative and competitive scheme of life. While the artist must be an adventurer and an experimenter and endeavor to shake off the shackles of the past and of convention, his purpose finally remains social, although it is personally expressed.

And so with the scientist. In science we have the best example of collaborative enterprise. The scientist has social responsibilities, because he has been brought up, fed, and maintained by society, just as his knowledge has come to him through thousands of social channels. The scientist who peers through a microscope to discover the new is beholden to the people who made the microscope, and he cannot move one single step without the help of the diffuse and organized co-operation of all mankind. Whatever he adds to knowledge has sooner or later a social significance, although it may not appear to have at the moment. A man need not seek an *immediate* purpose of his scientific labors, but he may be confident that sooner or later what he has discovered will fit into a useful scheme. Because some discoveries of science can be used to destroy the security and peace of the world, scientists are now trying to find ways of controlling their own products and preventing their use for antisocial purposes. Science cannot afford to be studiously aloof from the purposes for which its discoveries are used, else it becomes finally a curse to mankind rather than a blessing. What, for example, avails it for the psychiatrist to seek the means of curing individual madness when the men of science, of whom he is one, have helped foster mass madness?

Because man has built up storehouses of social attitudes, ideas, prejudices, skills, knowledge, and ways of life which are his psychological environment, ideas and prepossessions sweep in and out of him, just as air and foodstuffs do. His individuality lives only in the capacity to accept, to reject, and to select from the teeming, passionate, learned, hypocritical, zealous, custom-ridden, and custom-fighting world in which he lives.

Yet subjectivity, the feeling of individuality, is present in all of us. For all of us, at times, there is a loneliness that to so many is the real pain of living, a wall of separation that even in the densest crowds makes ghosts of one's fellows and an embodied nothing of oneself. There is a sense of selfhood when one views the world as from a distance, as I do now from my sickbed, knowing that I am mortally injured by the blocking of a little bundle of nerve fibers in my heart and that some day all the reality I now feel streaming into me will cease to be felt. Can I imagine at one and the same time my own disappearance and a still existent world?

Chapter IX

HEREDITY AND ENVIRONMENT

Man likes to dichotomize, to divide his problems into equal and opposing halves, so that he may glibly and easily discuss them. More relevantly and more cynically, this gives him an opportunity to express his impenitent partisanship, from cradle to grave to be in one camp or the other, fighting about everything under the sun. Thus he divides the world of values into absolute good and bad and sets up standards and slogans for which he fiercely fights and dies. He splits up the intricate universe into spirit and matter or, limiting his sphere to human life, into mind and body. It is as if the spectrum of reality were divided up only into black and white, and no consideration given to red, blue, yellow, and purple. Equally stringent is his division of the phenomena of life into heredity and environment.

Any separation between the hereditary forces and the total environment is artificial and is properly made only for purpose of convenience. It is true that Weismann was correct when he laid down his famous law that germ plasm — that is, the hereditary cells — build up the hereditary cells of the next generation; that there is a continuity, so to speak, of germ plasm throughout the generations and, consequently, throughout the whole of life. Certainly this is true if the evolutionary theory of life is true. But if it implies that the hereditary substance, the germ plasm, is isolated from the environmental forces and from the fate of the body as a whole, then it is decidedly not true.

Actually, the germ plasm is, in man and in animals like him, merely the active cells of the testes in the male and of the ovaries in the female, and the chromosomes and genes are the active genetic material of these cells. The body as a whole is bombarded and penetrated by chemicals and radiations of all kinds, which pass finally into the bloodstream and are carried by the blood, *the internal environment*, to every cell within the organism. In this way the cells of the germ plasm, like all the cells in the body, are nourished by chemicals in the form of primary foodstuffs and gases. The germ plasm is as dependent upon vitamins, which come from plants and other animals, as are the cells that support the germ plasm.

Withhold the gases and the foodstuffs, and the germ plasm dies. Change the character of the blood in a manner sufficient to change the metabolism of the body as a whole, and the germ plasm alters in its reactions. It may under such circumstances develop such individuals as cannot be born. Experiments carried out in some of the lower animals show that the nature of the offspring can be decidedly altered. There have even been many experiments which showed that powerful environmental forces can be so brought to bear on the germ plasm as to lessen its capacities to produce normal individuals for a considerable time.

I see no reason to believe that the bad environment

in which the majority of civilized men live, with its crowded and horrid slums, its deficient vitamins, its minus in wholesome living-conditions and its plus in destructive and disorganizing factors, is without effect on the sheer vitality of the cells of the testes and ovaries. No animal-breeder, however devoted to eugenics and breeding he might be, would place his cattle in overcrowded, dirty, airless chambers and, while underfeeding and overworking them, expect to raise prize-winners. No plant biologist, stressing as he properly does the hereditary factors as the road to new and finer plants, would exclude sun and water and plant his prized seed in deficient soil. It is an article of faith rather than of completely established fact to believe that the germ plasm may be more or less permanently affected and send out defective human beings generation after generation, but it is not a blind faith. Rather is it the as-if, the legitimate hypothesis of science, and one that needs application to human biology.

The constancy of the germ plasm, its capacity to reproduce in identical fashion generation after generation, is dependent not only on its own make-up but on the reaction of that make-up with the rest of the world. This does not mean that we know any way by which the environment can produce cats out of dogs, or make a black man into a white man. By experimental means, however, we can alter the proportion of the naturally expected sexes, as well as the size, weight, strength, agility, viability, and general excellence of the product. No matter how good the germ plasm may be, if there is not enough calcium in the food, the offspring have deficient bones.

This defectiveness may not continue generation after generation. But it certainly shows that the germ plasm as such is immediately dependent for its activities upon the environment. In fact, there is no such thing as germ plasm without environment; it is always germ plasm plus, minus, or times the environment.

The process of development from the egg to the fully developed individual is a succession, regular, orderly in type, of chemical and physical changes by which the primitive, one-celled creature becomes finally a differentiated multicellular living thing with departments of all kinds taking care of each function of the organism.

The original inborn tendency to do all this is called heredity; but the evolution itself, from the time of the fertilization on, is a *reaction process* taking place between the environment *in its totality* and the various forces unified under the one word "heredity." I have tried to find similes for all this and have failed. The hereditary substance might be called the dough and the environment the baker; but then you have to imagine a dough that can take on any one of a million shapes, yet successfully resist any attempt to change the particular and special shape. The development of one cell into a many-billioned-cell living human being is something like taking one grain of crude ore and from it evolving an automobile. Defects that are present in the earlier phases of the job produce early ruin, and the material and unfinished product are ruthlessly thrown away, like a two-week-old abortion. But this simile fails, too, since the living fetus manufactures its own workmen and engineers, as well as its own gears and carburetor.

Most discussions of heredity and environment exhibit the pugnacious human tendency to think that success in battle determines rightness and wrongness of belief; that skill in presentation — in other words, the debating quality — has something to do with the facts of any situation. Scientists are no exception to this universal trend. They readily take sides and proceed to battle under banners and slogans just as other folk do in the common affairs of life. Scientists also fall into the well of this fallacy, that when a new set of facts establishes a new theory, they tend to neglect the warnings of the history of thought and ideas and believe that truth has finally been established, and the whole truth at that. They then exaggerate the new set of facts and the consequent ideas into a universal explanation and fundament of phenomena. This has been peculiarly the case in the recent history of genetics and eugenics. The Mendelian hypothesis came along, and everything in genetics and biology was to be explained by Mendelism, which is decidedly not the case, although no one can deny and no one wishes to deny the greatness of Mendel.

The famous Mendelian hypothesis, stressing unit characters, explains only fragments of the hereditary phenomena. It explains the differences without accounting for the much more important similarities. Thus the smoothness or the roughness of the pod of the pea may be inherited as a unit character and expressed in Mendelian ratios. Similarly with the color of the pod, its greenness or yellowness. But the pod itself is *invariably* inherited and no Mendelian ratios are at all discernible. Moreover, the color and the smoothness of the pod,

which are inherited according to Mendelian laws, have
no fundamental relationship to the vitality of the pea or
to its essential character, let us say, of peaness. The pod
is essentially the same whether it be smooth or rough,
yellow or green. In other words, the Mendelian ratio explains a minor adjectival quality of the pea and not the
noun of its nature, which is an envelope made up largely
of cellulose enclosing the seed of a plant called the pea.
So in human beings the ratio of occurrence of blue and
gray eyes has been studied, and it has been more or less
established that Mendelian laws govern in a complicated
way the occurrence of blueness or grayness. But whether
the eye is blue or gray, the essential qualities of the
human eye are the same. Its eyeness is not at all Mendelian in occurrence.

Haldane points out that genetics is primarily concerned with variation, and says that "it is not possible to
give a reasonable answer to the question, 'Why are they
both mice? Why does a pair of mice produce another
mouse and not a rat or a motor-bicycle?' " It is curious
to note how alike human beings actually are, how inexorably the processes of a common heredity place the nose
at about the same relative position and give it a general
shape that is similar throughout mankind, differing only
in minor details. The essential biological processes upon
which life depends are nearly the same throughout the
world. It is interesting and thrilling to reflect that the
blood of man is almost identical wherever men are found,
and has a very slight variation from one human being
to another. And whether a man lives in the tropics or
up in the frozen north, his body temperature is within a

degree or a degree and a half of normal range. Even such a phenomenon as height has really a narrow range of variation. The difference between tall races and short races is a matter of a few inches. Five feet three inches is the height of a very small man. Six feet, which is nine inches more — only a slight proportion of the entire individual — is the height of a tall, almost gigantic man. When a man says "little woman" to his wife, the difference in height between him and her is usually about three inches, not enough to get excited about as indicating any startling difference in the two sexes. Yet as we watch our fellows, we pay a fascinated and critical attention to differences rather than to similarities.

If we look at human traits, we realize that there are hereditary gestures, hereditary methods of expressing sorrow, joy, disgust, and wonder throughout the human race. All men weep and all men laugh. Whether they say "Alas" or "*Weh ist mir*" is a superficial overlay of conventional type. The laughing-crying mechanisms stem from the same brain centers and have the same general constitution, just as the tears have about the same saltiness and run down the face in about the same way.

The point is that the essential biological, psychological, and social features of human beings are closely similar. The structure of the body, in those main and vital peculiarities upon which life depends in all people, is almost identical. Whether the nose be hooked or straight, flat or pointed, large or small is of no great importance so far as survival is concerned.

The chromosomes and genes are probably only a small part of the hereditary machinery by which the continuity and the sameness of any species is brought about. The egg-cell as a whole, with its intricate chemistry, is probably more important in so far as the main characters of the new individual are concerned. It is important to realize that *the female is in the main line of sexual reproductive development, with the male as an accessory before the fact, so to speak.* One of the great achievements of the renowned physiologist Jacques Loeb was to show that in some of the lower animals mere needling or chemical physical irritation of the female cell would stimulate it to reproduction independently of any sperm. Moreover, in the multicellular animals like man, the female furnishes within her own body the first great environment for the developing individual. During a nine-month period the fetus receives all the intricate and highly potent inner environment of the mother. This is probably the most important environmental influence of the whole life career of the new individual. When the child is born through the pains of maternal labor, it is nursed by the milk that the body of the mother has manufactured. It is quite typical of the rewards system of our society that the youngster takes the father's name, and that the father crowns the absurd arrogance of his position by saying: "She is the mother of my child."

It is not my purpose to make this a treatise on genetics. Certain it is, however, that no one can deal with the human being, whether in his sickness or his health, without being deeply impressed by the inexorable workings of the hereditary processes — that is, processes which seem to be independent of anything in the direct life circumstances of the individual himself. Our world of ideas would be shattered as if by an ideological earthquake if a cat gave birth to a dog, or if from the egg of a fish a bird developed. This would be a greater revolution than anything else we can possibly imagine. Moreover, if a cat were to suckle a puppy and raise the little biologic intruder with her own kittens, though she zealously taught him to stalk and to hunt in cat fashion, sooner or later his dogness would assert itself and he would finally be — a dog. He would not chase cats and some of his minor reactions would be changed, but his major physiology and psychology would be unaltered.

When one gets down to lesser things and sees, for example, the constant inheritance over generations of the shape of a nose, or the dread appearance of hemophilia; when one sees a breast tumor develop in each male of a whole line, or the fate-like occurrence of mental disease in brothers, sisters, parents, grandparents, uncles, and aunts; then no argument whatever will displace the importance of the hereditary processes, those processes which start with the fertilization of an egg by a sperm and go on to the evolution throughout life of the individual.

The term "heredity" relates to many processes and not to one. The term "evocative heredity" means that in response to a new and special type of environment special latent hereditary characters appear and are inherited in accordance to Mendelian ratios. For instance, it has been found that some plants decorate themselves with different colors, according to the amount of sunlight. Such a plant that is red in sunshine is green when it is grown in the shade; and so plants having the same genetic composition may produce red or green according to where they live. We also find that fruit flies, the miniature guinea pigs of science, develop a type of defective abdomen when they are raised in a moist laboratory. This characteristic is inherited regularly according to Mendelian sex-linked ratios. When the animal is transplanted to a dry laboratory, the defective abdomen disappears and the normal abdomen of the species is inherited regularly. The environment — that is, the moist laboratory — has not created the defective abdomen. The genes for its appearance are present, but *only express themselves in relationship to an evocative environment*. One might compare this evocative phenomenon to a paper written upon with invisible ink. The message remains without import or value until the heat of the environment is applied, and, lo, the latent becomes real, visible, and active.

If we apply the lesson of the fruit fly to *Homo sapiens*, we can, I think, state that possibly pathological characters or even normal ones appear only under evocative conditions. In a warrior age the social environment tends to evoke the warrior qualities of ferocity and hardihood and to crush the qualities that make for peaceful living. For example, in the earlier part of the Christian era the Scandinavians were a group whose very name was synonymous with piracy, freebooting, and savage warlikeness. Their very heaven, by its daily battles and its nocturnal orgies of overdrinking, exemplified their heart's desire. They ravaged the coasts of France, invaded England, swept into Italy, and conquered Sicily. According to the chronicles of the times, the Northmen were characterized chiefly by their robbery, rape, and desecration. Their descendants, however, are now among the most peaceful of European peoples and have a social history marked by compromise, liberalism, and general advance, without social discord or revolution. In modern Europe they are relatively small nations, and their warlike qualities are no longer evoked, while their peaceful qualities are. We need not assume that the contemporary "middle way" Swedes, Danes, and Norwegians have a biology and genetics different from those of their ferocious ancestors. As in our laboratory experiments, a marked change in environment can evoke some latent genetic characters, while inhibiting the expression of others.

When I was a boy, the great majority of American athletes were of Anglo-Saxon or Irish descent, with only an occasional German, Jew, or representative of some other people. But look at the names of the men on the successful football teams now. Races considered not at all athletic have their athleticism evoked by the American atmosphere, and so we see Slavs, Italians, and Jews as shining luminaries in football, baseball, and sports of all kinds. We also see that the most extraordinary athletes are Negroes, who, if this is a criterion of racial superiority, are probably the finest people on the face of the earth.

It would seem utterly unnecessary to prove that intelligence needs opportunity for its development, but the fanatical attitude of a large group of psychologists and geneticists obliges me to cite further examples of the obvious. There has been a great deal of work done on what

is called the innate intelligence of various racial groups.
The technique of proving that one racial group is superior
in intelligence to another is to compare either their
achievements or their scores in psychometric examinations.

Merely citing the achievements of a group hardly
proves their innate superiority. During the Middle Ages,
when the Arabs were the finest scholars and the best
scientists, such a study would easily have "proved" that
the Arabs were superior to any Teutonic or Nordic group.
Conclusions based on psychometric examinations are no
more reliable. Such a study made during the First World
War purported to show that the native white American
was innately superior to both immigrants and Negroes.
Curiously enough, the immigrants' inferiority was expressed quite clearly in a ratio corresponding to the length
of time the foreign group had been in the United States.
That this might relate to the Americanization of the immigrant and that the tests might be mere tests of adjustment to American culture, rather than of intelligence, did
not occur to these proponents of racial and group differences. Nor did they realize that the difference between
the Negro and the white was a difference of opportunity
rather than a difference in innate intelligence, though it
is obvious that the Negro has far less opportunity to acquire learning and to develop intelligence than the white.

Other people were not so completely convinced, and
a later study of whites and Negroes revealed results devastating to the theory of innate superiority. When the
Southern white was compared with the Northern Negro.
the following appeared:

Whites

Mississippi 41.25
Kentucky 41.50
Arkansas 41.55

Negroes

New York 45.02
Illinois 47.35
Ohio 49.50

On this basis the Northern Negro may be said to be superior in innate intelligence to the Southern white, although the Southern white on the whole is the descendant of such fine groups as the Scotch, the Irish, and the English and represents often the purest Anglo-Saxon blood in America. Ruth Benedict, commenting on this fact, said: "Obviously even the dominant White race did badly in the tests if they had been reared in certain Southern states, where per capita expenditures for education are low and the low standard of living is revealed in every survey and to every casual visitor."

Whatever criteria we have had for innate intelligence, whether it be the I.Q. or accomplishment, have been inadequate in the essentials for scientific evaluation. If any experiment is to be done to study the effect of any single factor, all other factors must be kept constant. If I am to test the effect of a drug on blood pressure, I must have the individuals to be tested in a basal condition — that is, one uniform state. I cannot compare one person who is active with another who is resting, nor an old sick man with a young strong one. To evaluate the new drug, all the variables must be kept as nearly constant as possible. If the factor of innate intelligence is to be weighed and a scientific conclusion reached, the educational opportunities, social advantages, social position, social traditions, health, and a thousand and one things that make for the fostering and developing of intelligence and accomplishment must be kept uniform.

The stuff out of which an individual is made can be and is molded by the physical and social environment into one shape or another. Any dichotomy between heredity and environment is artificial and misleading. While we come closest to the truth with the principle of evocative environment, we must always remember that one cannot make a steel tool out of wood; and also that no matter what happens to steel, it still remains a superior form of iron.

Chapter X

GENIUS

In any review of the hereditary factors and their interaction with environmental agencies we ought to consider
certain questions about genius. The term is difficult to
define, as the genius himself is often incomprehensible in
terms of his origin and in the more mysterious terms of
his deeds and capacities.

Is genius allied to madness, as Dryden put it? To his
servant the genius must seem unintelligible and at times
even definitely foolish, since the average man measures
men and things in terms of common sense and practicality, instruments that are valuable to mediocrity but that
may be unimportant to the genius. In Anatole France's
Crime of Sylvestre Bonnard, Hamilcar, the cat, compares
his master, the Academician, with the housekeeper:
"This old bookman talks to no purpose at all, while our
housekeeper never utters a word that is not full of good
sense, full of significance — containing either the an-
nouncement of a meal or the promise of a whipping. One
knows what she says. But this old man puts together a
lot of sounds signifying nothing."

To one for whom only the trivial details of the world
are important, the absorption of a contemporary genius
with his abstractions and his long immersion in frantic
and disheveled effort must seem ridiculous, if not sinister.

The stranger is always the object of suspicion, and the genius in a certain sense is the victim of xenophobia, since he tends to be a stranger even to those with whom he lives.

A group of workers, starting with Lombroso and his pupil Nordau, have attempted to show that genius is a form of degeneracy. But their studies are shot through with the fallacy of the positive instance. Because the man of genius was (and is) often mentally sick, or at least peculiar, therefore they prove their theses by citing the many cases of this kind.

One can mention a tremendous number of men of genius who were mentally sick or whose ancestors and relatives had a full share of alcoholism, mental disease, criminality, and peculiarity. Hans Andersen, for example, had a grandfather and father who were insane, and a mother who died of delirium tremens. Balzac was a hypomanic personality, or, in lay terms, he had a mental disease with ups and downs in mood; and his father had a depression of such severity that for twenty years, although not physically sick, he did not leave his bed. Beethoven, the prince of musicians, was quarrelsome and unreasonable and had a tendency to the use and abuse of alcohol; his father and grandmother are said to have been drunkards. Napoleon Bonaparte is declared to have had a neurotic father, a brother, Louis, who was definitely psychopathic, a sister, Pauline, who was a hypomanic, degenerated personality, and another brother, Jerome, who was characterized as unstable. Napoleon himself, declared to be a neurotic, was possibly suffering from epilepsy and narcolepsy.

Disease is difficult enough to diagnose during life and certainly impossible to diagnose from mythical and legendary statements. There is no doubt, however, that Byron, for example, was an abnormal personality, and the fact that his grandfather died by suicide may possibly be of importance. Dostoyevsky suffered from epilepsy and had a son who died from epileptic seizures. Goethe was a manic-depressive, and his life, if measured by ordinary terms, was psychopathic. Robert Mayer, famous physicist, the discoverer of the principle of the conservation of energy, suffered from manic-depressive insanity. He was hypomanic even when he conceived his important theory and was in an insane asylum for one year.

To know that Isaac Newton suffered from schizophrenia from his fiftieth year on does not help us to explain his greatness. His illness may account for the fact that he never married, and that he lived a life aloof from his family; and it undoubtedly gave solitariness to his genius. But it had nothing to do with his genius as such, and nothing to do with the discovery of the law of gravitation or his brilliant theories of light. It bore no relationship to his mathematical powers and to the triumphs of his intellect.

Edgar Allan Poe stands out as a prime example of the abnormal personality who enriches the world by his activities. His father was a psychopathic personality; one brother is said to have been a drunkard, one sister an idiot; and Poe himself was an alcoholic as well as a drug habitué. Let us concede that Poe was a drunkard and given to fits of depression. When he was depressed completely, he could not work. It was only as he recovered from his fits of depression that he wove into his design of life something of his experiences when depressed. His depressed state gave him a view of life, common enough among thousands of the melancholy, which only his genius could transmute into heart-rending beauty.

To select only one other, the great Leo Tolstoy had a grandfather who was psychopathic, in that he was superstitious and a gambler, borrowed money senselessly, undertook hundreds of things, and ruined himself and his relatives. Tolstoy himself is declared to have been a psychopathic personality with hysteric traits, who finally developed melancholia.

The trouble with all this is that while mental disease is everywhere, the white and brilliantly revealing light of publicity stays only on the eminent and distinguished. Their contemporaries watch them carefully, viewing them with derision as well as with admiration, since the human being is always divided in his attitude toward the great people around him. There is just as much, if not more, psychopathy, alcoholism, manic-depressive psychosis, epilepsy, and idiocy among the common people, but it is buried within their obscurity. The common man lives and dies in the darkness of the mass, or if there is any illumination on his life, it is that of a candle in the hands of those who actually meet him and know him. Only the novelist has really studied the common man, and he has found as much psychopathology among peasants and sailors as among the gifted. There is, in reality, no evidence that "great wits are sure to madness near allied."

A different but equally one-sided and misleading point

of view about genius is that represented by Galton and, after him, a long line of successors, mainly eugenists. These men have sought to prove that not only genius, which they have considered merely as eminence and high ability in the directions most rewarded, but societies have been based finally and fundamentally on heredity. They have studied inclusion in *Who's Who*, the number of professors in a family, the number of books written by them, and scientific and social recognition of them in general. They prove beyond a doubt, and this no one can question, that, in the main, men of eminence and genius spring from families in which eminence and ability have been evident for one or more generations. These proponents of the hereditary origin of great ability find the great Darwin family their best stock in trade. Certainly that he had a grandfather like Erasmus Darwin gives some clue to the origin and the ability of a Charles Darwin; for Charles Darwin to have as cousin Francis Galton impresses one deeply as a mark and unquestionable manifestation of the innate origin of high ability. From then on, however, the family tree is mainly one of eminence, and since eminence is social too, one great man can pull up his whole family. The start given in life, the associations, the trend and direction of activity by the acclaim and the prestige of one gifted individual are sufficient to pull mediocrities into a higher position than they would ordinarily occupy without that social favoritism. For social favoritism, social pull ("social graft," if one wants to use the term), is a constant and continuous force. It is easy to do favors for the sons and relatives of the eminent. They progress through life in a vehicle that has a motor power higher than ordinary, independent of the power of the passengers. The man who would be a failure if left to himself is carried along until he finally reaches stability and success; whereas without that continuous aid his early failures would condition his career to permanent disaster. Social favoritism cannot appear in statistics, and thus a statistical study is of little worth because it ignores such concealed, yet valid, oiling of the social machinery. The easier access to golden opportunities is a constant factor making for success. We can only say finally that great ability probably is innate; that eminence, however, may be merely a matter of opportunity.

In England the upper middle class shows a much higher rate of eminence than the lower middle class, but the caste system in England has been such that only exceptionally does an individual break into official position and real opportunity unless he and his forebears have gone to some "right" public school. Certainly there is more nepotism and social favoritism in financial success than in even the most graft-ridden politics. The man who himself has been successful surrounds himself with his relatives, who thereby get opportunities they could ordinarily not possibly obtain for themselves.

If a man who is born into a family of attainment does not succeed in maintaining his place, he is relatively feebleminded, and if he merely maintains his place, he is not much more than mediocre. *To rise above your original place is the test of greatness*, and most of these families of eminence show a definite regression from the place made for them by a few energetic and illustrious ancestors. The man who rises from obscurity to moderate success shows more ability than the man who slides from a place of highest eminence to one of lesser distinction, however great that diminished distinction may be. In other words, social bookkeeping must take into account the dynamics of favoritism.

Intensive studies have been done on what are known as gifted children, and the work of Terman and his associates in this country stands out as monumental in this respect. These works show a marked direction in the distribution of high scholastic ability; Jews and northern Europeans on the whole do best in the tests by which psychologists measure innate ability. The capacities measured by these psychological tests appear very early. Unfortunately, there is absolutely no reason to believe that the tests measure genius in the least. Time has yet to show that these so-called gifted children will do better than occupy professorial chairs, write a few books, hold leading places in finance, produce a few pictures, or create a few musical compositions. It is very doubtful that from them will come those who will electrify the world by original contributions.

In fact, the psychological tests are made up by people of a certain class or group who define intelligence in terms of their own abilities and capacities rather than those capacities which serve the world in the most fundamental way. If mechanics instead of professors of psychology devised intelligence tests, the sons and daughters of mechanics would show up much better than the doctors', merchants', and lawyers' children who now occupy the leading places in the psychometric examinations. It all reminds one of the story about the lion who, wander-

ing through a picture gallery, saw a great painting of a
hunter spearing a lion and said: "Ah, if lions painted pictures . . ." The mechanics whose efforts support our
present world do not frame tests of ability; nor do farmers
or laborers. We must always remember that when we get
into the field of social conclusion, which this is, we deal
with caste, class prejudices, and cultural compulsives
both subtly and directly corruptive of reality.

Nobody who believes in the innate capacities of children and who decries the environment as a factor of
great importance acts according to his ideas. He surrounds his children with the very best influences that
he can possibly procure for them. He is extremely careful
of their food and their rest. Even though he may say:
"The doctors are poisoning the race by keeping alive the
unfit," he seeks the best medical advice. He does not
rely on innate talent, but starts his children's musical
education early and with the best masters he can afford.
He does not, if he can help it, live in a crowded tenement
district, but seeks the sunshine and open air, the physical and mental vitamins of life, as assiduously as he can,
so as to bring them to his own little brood. His deeds
contradict his theories in every matter of his daily and
lifelong attitude toward his own. This is of importance,
since it indicates an instinctive something that may be
more valid in the final analysis than any cold statistics.
This is not to say that the truly gifted child is not so
born. He is so born. Truly gifted parents may produce
gifted children — but not so commonly as is supposed —
and in such households there is always the tragedy of the

children who do not live up to their opportunities and their social expectations.

Because Galton's studies omit by some strange chance the failures, the psychotic, the psychopathic, the criminalistic, the feebleminded, and the epileptic, his work is as misleading as Lombroso's. One finds no record of mental disease and feeblemindedness among these distinguished groups. This cannot be the case, unless English distinction is biologically different from American distinction. I headed a group that studied certain great American families, families whose names are incorporated in the very warp and woof of American achievement and form part of the legend and tradition of American life. As we delved into hospital records and unearthed the bald statements incorporated in probate courts, we found among these families mental disease galore, yet the genealogies of these great American families made no mention of those members who had been incarcerated in hospitals for mental disease or adjudged insane by a court. So far as the family tree was concerned, every apple that hung from it was luscious and red. The complete records told a story of considerable decayed and distorted fruit.

One of the greatest of American philosophers, a man most closely connected with the whole tradition of American letters and distinguished by the warmth and brilliancy of his genius, had two brothers sufficiently sick mentally to be in hospitals. A great psychologist, who described himself in his own writings and pictured most movingly his deep and dark moods of depression, had a brother institutionalized with a melancholia. It suffices to state that one family group that has been held out as a contrast to feebleminded groups of classical fame (such as the Jukes and Kallikaks) had a considerable amount of mental disease that does not appear in the family's genealogies. I now have a very cynical attitude toward all genealogies. They tend to list only the assets and omit all the liabilities of the family name. Since they are miracles of disingenuousness, if not of mendacity, they usually have little value for science.

The fallacy of the family name obscures thinking in all genealogical studies, whatever purpose underlies them. The family name passes down from male to male, generation after generation, but the Smiths of the first generation are akin to the Smiths of the fourth generation mainly by tradition and the family name and perhaps social standing. The germ plasms of the various Smiths have stemmed from a thousand sources and are mixed in inextricable and very dissimilar fashion from the first to the fourth generations.

The mental illness in these great families was mainly manic-depressive psychosis, although there was a scattering of other diseases. This is to say nothing of the unrecorded nervous breakdowns that occur everywhere and are really mental disease akin to manic-depressive psychosis. If these could be taken into account, the mental disease of these distinguished groups would have been appalling and might lead to the conclusion that there is a relationship between distinction, genius, and mental disease. But, unfortunately for this conclusion, *a control study done of undistinguished American groups showed*

*no essential difference in the amount of mental disease of
the same general types.*

So genius is not akin to madness. The madman may
be a genius and the genius a madman. These are largely
matters of coincidence, or, at the most, a little flavor is
given to the soup of greatness by the salt of abnormality.
The vitamins and the calories of genius are not created
by madness, nor have they anything real to do with it.
Indeed, when one studies the lives of men of scientific
genius, one finds a strangely normal group, one might say
even abnormal in their normality. Their lives are organized and their purposes seem clear. Their emotions seem
well controlled. Even sexuality, that cataclysmic dis-
turber of inner and outer tranquillity and of purpose, is
without precedent for regularity and steadiness in the
history of their lives. They are human, it is true, but the
liability to err, which is so strongly human a trait, is
much less manifest in their cases than in those of so-
called average men. It is only when we turn to men of
genius in art and literature that a disproportionate amount
of psychopathy seems to appear. But here we are in a
phase of life in which emotional expression, and personal
feeling of the tragedy and mysteries of existence, are
essential.

In no discussion of genius can we ignore the interaction of heredity and environment. The right man must
live at the right time and in the right place in order to be
a genius. Certainly Benjamin Franklin could never have
discovered the electric nature of lightning if Gilbert and
many, many others had not preceded him. Pasteur could
not have established the germ theory of disease if the

microscope had not previously been invented. Many other able men, however, immersed in the same currents of thought and information, lacked that extra bit of penetration and insight which distinguished Franklin and Pasteur.

Had Mozart been born into a world lacking musical culture or musical instruments, probably no one would have suspected that he was a Mozart, a potential master of music. Had Einstein lived in a pastoral world, where there were no physics and no mathematics, most likely he would have lived and died an unknown and perhaps an inferior member of his group, since his latent Einsteinness would not readily lend itself to physical hardihood, mental passivity, gross superstition, and the practicality of the everyday life of shepherds. In both these men the fortunate blending of inherited qualities would have been without importance had they lived at the wrong time or place. A card-player dealt four deuces will find them of great value if he is playing poker, of no value at all if he is playing bridge.

Whenever one notes the great influence of the individual genius, one is tempted to say that personality rules the world. A little deeper delving into the human terrain, and one sees personality expressing itself forcibly, beautifully, successfully, and cogently only "when the times are ripe." It is true that "there is a time and tide in the affairs of man," for only then can the great man embark on his journey.

Chapter XI

SURVIVAL OF THE FIT

The "cultural compulsive," as Calverton phrased it, is the bias given to theories and ideas by the interests, training, and motivations of the individual. There is a different cultural compulsive for Catholic and Protestant, for Jew and gentile, for rich and poor, for man and woman, and for all intermediates in religion, race, social position, and sex. This cultural compulsive is interestingly and exasperatingly shown in all or nearly all discussions on heredity and environment.

In Nazi Germany the established cultural compulsive was that of race and, therefore, birth and blood. Thus heredity became by far the most important factor in social biology, and the German studies on identical twins stressed only the fact that these mirror-image duplicates tend to be alike in their development. In Russia, since the economic basis of history is the all-in-all of the Communist ideology, the cultural compulsive is entirely focused on the environment. Thus it is proclaimed that the environment is, practically speaking, the all-important factor in the development of human beings, with the conditioned-reflex studies of Pavlov stressed as the basis of the evolution of the individual. Russian studies of identical twins point out the differences between them rather than their similarities.

The hereditarians tend, on the whole, to believe in racial purity; they are conservative and have a firm faith that those who fail are the unfit. They view and point out with alarm that the unfit people are prolific and the fit have a low birth rate. This seems to them to portend the end of the world and that "unless something is done about it, the race is going to the dogs." On the other hand, the environmentalists seem to believe that if cats gave birth to kittens in a stove, the offspring would be biscuits. They explain away hereditary differences and attribute the unfit modifications of human beings to underfeeding, disease processes, poverty, and unfavorable life conditions in general, so accounting for the deficient, the criminalistic, the psychotic, and, generally speaking, the failures and the "underprivileged" in life.

I still remember the chaos that burst into my purposes and ideals when, in my twenty-seventh year, a biologist whom I greatly respected said that the effects of the progress of medicine could be summarized as individual betterment and race degeneration. He believed that by keeping alive the unfit we doctors were allowing those who would naturally die early to survive and pollute the race with their weakness and pathology. He felt that eugenical sterilization was harsh, but necessary and preventive; that euthenics, which aims at eliminating the struggle for existence and helping the underdog, was therefore racially destructive. As for medicine, my chosen lifework, he called it the chief instrument in the philanthropic bedevilment of the human race, and said that each of its triumphs was a blow to the evolution of a successful human species.

More important biologists than my friend have used the concept of "natural selection" as an argument against ameliorative measures for the ills of human life. Malthus, believing that the birth rate is disproportionate to the rate of the means of subsistence, stated that if a man cannot get subsistence from his parents or cannot find a market for his labor, he has no right to live. Darwin said: "With savages the weak in body or mind are soon eliminated, and those that survive commonly exhibit a vigorous state of health. We civilized men, on the other hand, do our utmost to check the process of elimination. . . . We must therefore bear the undoubtedly bad effects of the weak surviving and propagating their kind." By saying that nature has no pity and seeks only survival of the fit, these men gave intellectual support to all those who decry tenderness in human relationships.

For my own satisfaction I have had to answer a great question: Is social amelioration and betterment a good for that something called the human race, or is there a final irreconcilable quarrel between eugenics, which aims at race betterment, and euthenics, which seeks to establish a kindlier and more reasonable world?

The idea of chemotherapy entered the world with the first herb doctor who distilled some leaves and roots into a potion to cure the ills of his fellows. That concept has in our day culminated in the manufacture of the marvelous sulfa compounds, which magically cure infections, halt pneumonia in its tracks, and transform gonorrhea into a minor ailment. Does this help the unfit to survive and thus pollute the human scene with weaklings? Did the development of dentistry lower the vitality of man and bring into life more people with decayed teeth? Or did it merely enable more people to smile and eat? Does the conquest of disease, the elimination of smallpox, the prevention of epidemics of cholera, dysentery, and typhoid, the progressive diminution of the incidence of tuberculosis help the unfit to survive? Or may it be a means by which the fit also are enabled to live out their lives and do their work in the world?

If we include medicine with human effort of a wider range, we may ask: do those efforts which seem most truly human and which spring from kindliness, gentleness, and tender feeling work against the race as a whole, soften it, and pave the way for its final disappearance or its unhappy survival as misbegotten, ill-endowed hordes of unfit? When we plan good houses, when we seek to prevent industrial accidents, when we lessen the hours of labor, when we see to it that each child is born with good care and fostered properly from his infancy onward, when we vote for governmental supervision of food, clothing, and shelter, when we seek to provide vacations, when we endeavor to reform the criminal, when we seek to change the economic structure so that there shall be no wage slavery and the laborer shall be given more than the bare subsistence that the "iron" law provides, are we then injuring the race?

The answer, so far as I am concerned, is decidedly no! These efforts are not merely euthenic, they are eugenic, too. In the first place, there is no proof that epidemics have any notion of what we call fit and unfit. Epidemics have no morals. They do not of necessity tend to involve the low-grade mentally and physically. The great influ-

enza epidemic of 1918 and 1919 showed no discrimination; it struck in the Army cantonments among the selected men of the race at least as heavily as it did in the
insane asylums and the schools for the feebleminded.
The fit who survive in such a situation are merely those
who either receive the infection in less virulent form or
possess some peculiar chemical composition utterly independent of their social and human values. Resistance to
most diseases is an individual peculiarity bearing no relationship to other values of the individual, those values
which we as human beings call good, moral, beautiful.

True, the undernourished and the overcrowded are
more apt to be involved in epidemics. Yet when an epidemic really gets going, there is no isolation, and all the
artificial barriers of separate homes and retreat into sequestered places help little, if at all. When a child lives
in a poor neighborhood, it is not his fault; nor is it a
measure of his own unfitness. A rat will survive an epidemic that men won't. In fact, a rat does not succumb
to a plague that it carries and that kills humans very
quickly. Under such circumstances the rat has a higher
fitness for survival, but who is hardy enough to say that
it is more fit to survive in general and more human
terms? A group of rats might well say that the diseases
that *carry them off* (and there are such diseases), but
to which man is immune, prove that the unfit survive,
and rat biologists might well build mighty theses around
this fact.

So the resistance to germs certainly has no bearing on
fitness as a whole. The rate of morbidity of any group
may measure its lesser exposure; it does not measure its

greater human fitness. Whatever we know of germ or virus diseases and whatever we do to conquer them have no bearing on the survival of the fit, if this term means the survival of the intelligent, the capable, the well-organized, the useful, and the creators of knowledge and beauty. In sober fact, the advent of sulfanilamide, arsphenamine, diphtheria antitoxin, and the many weapons of therapeutics, as well as those of preventive medicine, means just this in terms of racial welfare: that for one "unfit" who is helped to survive, a score of the fit are enabled to live out their lives and to beget their kind.

Man is a mosaic of qualities, fit qualities existing side by side with unfit ones. A man may get bald early and so have "unfit" hair, but his brain is not affected by the baldness of his skull. So a man with poor teeth may have great ability, and the dentist helps society by prolonging the period of this man's usefulness.

The discerning reader need only consider the countries where euthenics exists and those where it is lacking for the answer to come. Norway, let us say before the Nazi occupation, was a country where euthenics prevailed, where the sick were adequately cared for, the poor relieved from the crushing burden of their poverty, where housing programs were eliminating slums, where a paternalistic government (curious that the term "fatherly government" should be a term of reproach!) built up facilities for the distribution of vitamins and calories, for vacations spent in the open air, as well as for education of the underprivileged. China, on the other hand, was a country where no such efforts could be discerned or, more fairly, where they had just been started. Wherever one went in China, one saw the crippled, the blind, the scrofulous. The people, almost all undernourished and crowded together in miserable masses, were stunted, poorly organized folk, whose capacity for survival was on the lowest possible plane — that is, survival with misery, ignorance, and superstition. Now, there is no evidence that the Norwegian is *innately* a better biological specimen than the Chinaman. Yet a group of Norwegians compared with a group of Chinese would show stronger, cleaner, more capable, and better biological specimens. A study of these countries certainly gives no evidence that amelioration, medical effort, and euthenics in general injure the individual human being or the human race. Despite the claims of the pessimists, all the signs point in the opposite direction.

Far more important than the direct results of ameliorative effort are the indirect but enormously potent side-effects. As chemists, biologists, sanitary engineers, and medical men co-operate to conquer diseases, their joint labors bring to mankind that knowledge — for example, of vitamins and hormones — which is transforming the size, strength, and appearance of mankind. The six-foot giant of former days is a commonplace, moderately tall man of our times. Sun-baths and cod-liver oil have made the rickety, bowlegged child a relative rarity. The wise, more deliberate choice of foods has reduced the numbers of the starved and the fat alike. Euthenics, let us say the kindly spirit seeking to save the individual, develops an impartial science which, in its turn, makes possible a really better race.

Nor does this apply only to the body. We hear much

about the marvelous Greeks of the Golden Age, and yet we know nothing of their intelligence except that a cluster of great men appeared for a very short time. Paradoxically, our times produce fewer great men because there are more men of the first class. Aristotle could govern the thought of men for centuries just because there were few intellects really at work. Whenever we get the opportunity to study the intelligence of those who live under conditions at all similar to those of ancient Greece or medieval Britain, we find that it is less than that of the people who live where euthenics flourishes and educational opportunity exists.

There is one gross fallacy underlying all theories of the survival of the fit. If fitness means *only* survival, those who survive are fit, and the fit are those who survive in a specific environment, and so we come to a high-sounding statement that ultimately proves nothing. Thus an absent-minded scientist would die if he had to compete with a gangster on a desert island; and if a snake and a man were thrown into a well, it would not be the man who was fitter to survive. Moreover, it still needs demonstration that if the tender spirit disappeared, other cementing social influences would still survive. I think not, and believe that tenderness and kindness are necessary correlatives of lasting group co-operation.

There is in reality nothing nonnatural under the sun. Man is not something separate from nature, but a part of it, and the humanitarian spirit may be as fundamentally biological as the harsher attitude which declares that tenderness is not part of biology. Man's thinking and belief, however sharply they contrast with what goes on in the animal world, are an expression of man's biology, if we use that term in its broadest sense. Euthenics, and the spirit that makes it possible, are not sending the race to the dogs. Doctor and social worker, biochemist and reformer, and all the agents and agencies that seek quite directly to follow the social humanitarian instincts need not halt or lessen their efforts. Pasteur, Koch, Ehrlich, and their followers need not fear the criticism and the evaluation of Malthus, Darwin, Galton, and those who have echoed their words.

CHAPTER XII

STERILIZATION

However we may wish to improve the human race by kindly measures, we cannot overlook the existence in our midst of individuals markedly unfit to live in society. Many of these people cannot care for themselves or their children and are a burden to their families or their communities. There is also the possibility that their defects are hereditary, and that allowing these people to have children will result in spreading their disabilities even more widely through future generations. Naturally, the hereditarians, tending to be eugenists, favor sterilization, while the environmentalists point out the weakness of eugenical dogma and (proving that biases as well as politics make strange bedfellows) join with the Catholic Church in condemning sterilization.

Sterilization is a very simple operation. It can be performed on the male under local anesthesia and involves no hospitalization. It is merely cutting the little tubes that carry the sperms from the testicles to the penis. The operation not only does not prevent the sexual act but was devised by Steinbeck to increase potency in men who had lost it. Furthermore, since the testes remain intact, this operation is entirely different from castration, which makes the individual a eunuch, markedly changed in his sexual psychological constitution. In the female the sterilization operation is somewhat more difficult, although it is similar in its general principles. The Fallopian tubes, which carry the eggs from the ovary to the uterus, can be cut and the ends sewed up. Consequently the ova cannot reach the uterus and therefore cannot be fertilized by the sperms of the male. This is an abdominal operation, but not fundamentally serious, and within the capacity of a moderately skilled surgeon. Like male sterilization, it does not change the sexual nature in any significant degree. The internal secretion of the ovaries, the secretion by which femaleness is preserved, is not at all diminished. The menstrual periods continue and the nature of the woman is not altered. The sterilizing operation is not harmful to the health of either men or women, does not deprive them of the sexual relationship, but achieves the racial-social purpose of excluding those declared unfit for reproduction from achieving this purpose of their bodies.

It is much simpler to perform the operation of sterilization than it is to decide on whom the operation shall be done. There are those who advocate sterilizing *all* individuals who are "socially inadequate *by reason of heredity*," and here they include all the insane, the feebleminded, the epileptic, and certain chronic criminals. They assume that all these defects *are* hereditary and that individuals in these classifications are potentially the parents of defective offspring. They believe that such a program is needed if we are to prevent the unfit of our race from swamping the fit.

Thanks mainly to their efforts and to the celebrated dictum of Justice Oliver Wendell Holmes that three generations of imbeciles are enough, in this country there now are twenty-nine states that have laws providing in some way for the sterilization of the socially inadequate. The laws, although aiming at the same target, vary greatly in their specifications. Almost all of them provide for the sterilization of the feebleminded and the insane, several for the sterilization of the epileptic, and some for the sterilization of the habitual criminal and the syphilitic. Most of them apply only to the inmates of state institutions, but some apply also to individuals at large in the community or confined in private institutions. In some states these laws are "voluntary," in other states "compulsory."

The first sterilization law in America was passed by the Pennsylvania legislature in 1905, but it was vetoed by the Governor. The first sterilization laws still in effect were introduced in 1909 in California, Washington, and Connecticut. Following this, sterilization statutes were adopted in rapid succession by a number of states. Many of these laws were enacted without any definite program. They were frequently revised or amended, sometimes vetoed, and in many instances fell into disuse. Some of them have never really been put into effect, and the number of operations performed is so small as to be negligible. In Connecticut, for example, where the law is "compulsory," in the course of all these years the number sterilized each year averages thirteen, which indicates that the compulsion is not compelling and that the law is practically inoperative. California has almost as many sterilizations on record as the rest of the United States put together, and is the only state in the country that to any extent really enforces its sterilization law. Yet even in this state, with an average of about four hundred cases a year, the application of the law is limited when compared to the extent of the problem.

Those who consider these sterilization laws wise may ask why the enforcement is so lax. The answer is merely that in the United States there is formidable opposition to eugenical sterilization. In a democracy only those laws which have their bases in folkways or the approval of the strong groups have a chance of being enforced. The fate of prohibition demonstrates the futility of trying to make a drastic change in deeply embedded traditions. As for meddling with the sexual organs, there is a deep-seated repugnance which is socially instinctive and could be overcome only by great force or very intensive social education.

Before we reach any conclusions about these laws, about whether they should be enforced and whether similar laws should be enacted in other states, we should consider separately each of the conditions for which sterilization is advocated and see in which of them the hereditary factors *are* of importance.

In the first place come the mental diseases. That there are in the United States alone millions of people suffering from mental illness is to list just one consideration, and the staggering cost of caring for them is a second. The third consideration is measured in melancholia, delusion, and dementia, which are not expressed by statistics but weigh down hearts, bow heads, and crush the personalities not only of the sick but of their families. Nothing so breaks into the lives of the well as the mental diseases of those with whom they live; nothing so hurts the pride or arouses such devastating inner conflict. Accompanying the sympathy is the recoil of incomprehension and horror, and underneath the surface loyalty there is often deep, impatient disaffection. To love and care for the mentally disturbed is the final test of endurance, and so deep a drain on emotional reserve as to be beyond the powers of most normal people. There is a grim reason for the old term "alienist" to denote the man who looks after those felt to be aliens on the human scene.

Of course, insanity or mental disease is no unified thing. There are several mental diseases of various biological nature, each having different causes, courses, and possibilities for treatment, as well as totally differing relationships to heredity. "All cats look gray in the dark." When little was known, all the mental diseases were unified under the term "insanity." It is somewhat as if one labeled a disease "cough," not taking into account that cough as a symptom might arise from throat irritation, tuberculosis, pneumonia, bronchitis, irritation of the gastrointestinal tract, or emotion. The separation of the mental diseases into various groups represents the arduous and incomplete labors of many distinguished men. Scientific classification necessarily precedes the study of cause and often of cure.

Some mental diseases are comparatively easy to classify. The symptoms are uniform. There are identifiable physical signs and changes in the body during life, and finally autopsy reveals changes in the brain and other structures. Numerically the two most important of these are diseases consequent upon the changes of old age and due to alteration in the brain. In the first condition the arteries of the brain become narrowed and hardened, and the resultant damage to the nutrition of the brain brings the disease known as *arteriosclerotic dementia*. In the second condition certain structures called senile plaques or nodules develop in the brain, destroy the brain cells, and interfere with the brain function. This is called *senile dementia*. In both these diseases there is a failure in memory, intelligence, and judgment; a dilapidation of personality; marked physical signs of weakness or paralysis; and failure of the sensory functions such as vision and hearing. In some institutions for mental disease arteriosclerotic dementia and senile dementia constitute nearly forty per cent of the hospital population, yet these diseases exemplify no hereditary process we can do anything about. No one has as yet been hardy enough to suggest that we take steps to prevent the propagation of those who, after a useful lifetime, will become a burden to society at sixty or seventy years of age.

An important mental disease definitely due to physical changes within the brain is *general paresis*, or, to put it more precisely, syphilis of the nervous system and, more especially, of the brain. Ten to twenty years after the patient has contracted syphilis, he may develop a characteristic mental disease. Because syphilis is usually acquired early, the sufferers from syphilitic mental disease are involved at the height of their maturity. The diagnosis of syphilis can now be made by a laboratory chemist or assistant who has never seen the patient at all, and probably the understanding of general paresis or of neurosyphilis is the most precise achievement of psychiatry.

Without syphilis there is no general paresis. There is no known heredity to general paresis. This disease is of environmental origin only, at least for any practical purposes.

Another disease that is created by social, not individual heredity is most alcoholism. While it is true that a good many alcoholics are neurotic and that some suffer from depression, the main trouble with the alcoholic is that society not only permits him to buy without restriction a drug that he cannot handle, but even applies an extraordinarily potent social pressure to encourage its use. I am not a prohibitionist and certainly I believe that pleasure is a legitimate aim of man but, considering the enormous harm alcohol does, I believe that society should alter its traditional attitude toward drinking and forbid the sale of alcohol unless it is advertised honestly as a potentially dangerous drug.

We come next to schizophrenia and the manic-depressive states, the two great mental diseases still without any known physical signs and without any differentiating pathology and chemistry. Because the diagnosis is more or less empirical, whatever is said about the heredity of these diseases is not certain. Until a condition can be defined in exact terms, the question of its heredity remains as insecure as the clinical understanding of the disease itself. The reader must remember that we are far from any knowledge that would warrant the blatant dogmatism in most of the popular and some of the more scientific literature about the inheritance of the mental diseases. As one reads the eugenists, one would think that mental disease is clearly defined and well understood and, consequently, can be evaluated as to its heredity. That is decidedly not so.

These diseases are popularly classified as insanity. But "insanity" is only a legal term, meaning that the patient is in such a condition that the law must enter officially and control his property to conserve it against his own disordered judgment, or place him in custodial care to safeguard him and society. In both schizophrenia and the manic-depressive states, there are varying degrees of illness, as, for example, there are in tuberculosis. A man may have a patch of tuberculosis on one lung and live for a long time, or he may even be completely cured. On the other hand, he may have such marked breakdown of lung and other tissue that he dies quickly. In between these extremes of infection there are almost innumerable gradations. So a man may have schizophrenia and yet be able to maintain some kind of place in society; and most people who have a manic-depressive state never reach institutions and are never classified among the insane.

Generally speaking, schizophrenia tends to start early in life as a personality type that develops into disease. The past history of the schizophrenic is usually that of a shut-in, overmeticulous, overscrupulous personality. He has a certain stiff shyness that marks him off from other men. He (or she) has little successful sexual urge of an outer type; he may and does brood about sex, and is often in what I have called a sexual stew, but frequently nothing comes of this except masturbation. He may have peculiarities of conduct, rigidities and mannerisms of extreme type.

From this schizoid personality, the sick man descends

gradually or suddenly into a retreat from life. This retreat
is based on a falsification of his relationship with others.
He may believe that he is being persecuted. He misinter-
prets the irrelevant acts of other people and believes that
a stranger who looks at him as he passes will make an
adverse criticism and communicate this unfavorable opinion to others, perhaps will consider him homosexual or
vile in some other way, or even will follow him to do him
damage. While the normal person takes refuge in the
certainty that what goes on inside his head is known only
to himself, unless he communicates it, the schizophrenic
loses this feeling of safety and thinks that others know
and read his mind. He feels that he is no longer able to
do what he could before: to think consecutively, feel
vividly, and act without constraint. He may then develop
a "delusion of influence," a belief that somehow an influence of mysterious and potent nature is being used on
him by others — The Others. For he is now an alien in
the world.

It is interesting that the nature of this influence
changes with each cultural level and scientific achievement. In the days when men believed in "possession" by
demons and witches, the schizophrenic claimed that he
was bewitched and possessed. Later, when hypnosis was
widely discussed and its powers were greatly exaggerated,
hypnotism was the instrument of influence. As physical
scientific devices developed and it became possible to
talk and see at a distance, the radio and television became
the means by which others influenced the schizophrenic.
The mechanism of projection, which creates scapegoats
for us all, is strongly evident in this disease. The schizo-

phrenic finds that his difficulties are created by others, either concretely as coming from one person or group, or vaguely as coming from "Them."

So the schizophrenic lives his life in a brooding, silly, grimacing, retreated fashion. Either he becomes over-passive, submitting without any protest to whatever his caretakers do to and for him, or else he becomes senselessly resistive, fighting any effort to change him even from one place in a ward to another. And there also appears as part of the symptomatology of this disease the transformation of one's own thoughts into voices or hallucinations of one type or another.

The disability inherent in this disease is enormous. The course may run from a short episode that never recurs to a chronic progressive disorder that only grows worse as life goes on, although there may be sharp remission, in which the individual seems much better.

No pathology, no specific altered physiology, has been discovered, although the patients as a whole become inferior in physique and disordered in physiology as time goes on. This is no wonder, since they live aloof from all the invigorating recreative activities of man. In the institutions many of them work, but since they have no spontaneity and little initiative, they need constant spurring and guidance. Too many of them slip into a state that can only be described as vegetating; they may sit or stand all day in some fixed posture, absorbed in a sort of vacuum; or they may groove their activities in a senseless, stereotyped succession.

Before considering the heredity of this disease, let me turn to the other great mental disorder of unknown physiology and pathology, the *manic-depressive* state. The term "manic-depressive" means that the individual alternates between a state in which he is overexcited, elated, overactive, and usually overjoyous and one in which he shows the opposite mood of grim depression. In the manic state he may be merely over-gay, overtalkative, superficial in his speech, and given to punning. He may even be the life of the party, highly amusing when the condition is still under control. In fact, many individuals go through life in what is known as the hypomanic state; that is, they are manic, but never completely lose control. They never feel fatigue and are indomitable; while they tend to pass from one interest and excitement to another, they may even achieve great things and be notable in their lifework. One may even envy the individual in a hypomanic state, since his emotions are all charged with champagne and his energies are almost inexhaustible. But unfortunately the full manic stage often supervenes, and then the fantastic euphoric conduct, the recklessness, and the complete breakdown of inhibition force society to incarcerate the patient in a hospital, to save himself and others from disaster.

From this overcharged condition he may and usually does pass into the opposite state of depression. He experiences deep melancholy and complete failure of enthusiasm and energy, and loses his sense of reality and his feeling of the worthwhileness of life. From time to time, as we uneasily scan our lives, all of us suffer from a sense of guilt; but the melancholiac feels this in so magnified a form that he accuses himself not only of complete unworthiness but of unforgivable sin, of having created the disasters of the world. He believes that because of his guilt those whom he loves will be punished in one way or another by man or by God. The bluest blue mood of the normal person is a bright rainbow compared to the hopeless darkness of the manic-depressive patient. Losing the will to live, he may have only the desire to die. Suicide often ends the career of the manic-depressive patient.

The milder depressive cases are the bane and the perplexity of those who deal with them. They are adjured from morning to night to "snap out of it" and are given all kinds of banal advice. If they are overactive, they are told to rest more. If they show a tendency not to meet others, they are exhorted to be more social, when the very will to be social has been paralyzed. The patent fact that the "good advice" is impossible to follow does not lessen the stream of irritating importunity.

There is a very strong tendency to recover spontaneously from the manic-depressive state. The attacks may be long and violent, or short and not too greatly disturbing. The patient may need incarceration in an institution or, on the other hand, may even continue at work throughout the whole of life.

The metrazol and later the electric-shock method have become of great use, especially for the depressive state. They produce really miraculous recoveries, but recoveries only in the sense of cutting short the individual attack, for unfortunately the disease tends to recur.

Disease knows no favorites. Schizophrenia and the manic-depressive state occur among the rich and poor, the bright and dull, Jew and gentile, black and white.

Despite all that has been done, no substantial physiology or pathology has been established for these illnesses. The prevailing opinion is that they are mainly constitutional and hereditary. Although the environment may have some bearing on the breakdown and certainly colors the beliefs and attitudes of the patient, the main and basic factor is an inborn vulnerability or predisposition. To this I subscribe with certain reservations based on the fact that where little is really known and definitely established, little can be dogmatically stated.

There is not much precise value in saying that a condition is hereditary if one cannot say what machinery of the organism is involved. If we speak of the inheritance of diabetes, we are at least able to say that the cause of diabetes is some as yet unknown disturbance of the pancreas-pituitary function whereby the body cannot properly utilize sugar. Here a fairly precise mechanism and disturbance in this mechanism can be easily studied in parents, children, and relatives. Quite different are these mental diseases which cannot be well defined. Even when the patient is under study, there may be a great difference of opinion as to the diagnosis, and when we attempt to compare this more or less nebulous understanding with something equally unknown in the parent, we find that there is no basis for any dogmatism about the inheritance of mental illness.

The statistics, however, indicate altogether too great a proportion of cases occurring in family groups, among brothers and sisters and the close of kin to be coincidental. Of course, if one extends the idea of the family to include uncles, aunts, and first cousins, mental disease will be found in every family group. Yet while there are sporadic cases in every family, in some families the sprinkle becomes the shower. So for the present, even though we do not know the mechanism by which heredity operates in these cases, we can say that it is the most important single factor involved.

This is borne out by a study of those touchstones of the operation of heredity and environment, identical twins. When one twin has schizophrenia or a manic-depressive state, the liability of the other to have the same disease is enormously greater than mere chance, although there are cases where one such person has the disease and his twin does not develop it. The term "concordance" has been invented to express similarity of fate in identical twins. *The concordance of schizophrenia and the manic-depressive state in identical twins, while not one hundred per cent, is so great as to leave almost no doubt that a hereditary factor is involved.*

It is worth while considering the statement that the insane are increasing in our population. For several generations the commitment rate to institutions increased, as would naturally be expected. If a community has no hospitals and then starts building them, the commitment rate goes up as each hospital is built and as there are more facilities to take care of the insane and the defective. Communities that are backward in other ways do not feel the need for institutions. Thus the paradox: *low-grade communities have few hospitals and a low commitment rate. High-grade communities, sensitive to hospital needs, build hospitals and have a high commitment rate.* In a community that has as many institutions as it needs and desires, the commitment rate remains stationary or even drops. This is true in many countries and in Massachusetts and New York, the two most carefully studied states in this country. In this type of community the only increase in commitment rate has been in the senile and arteriosclerotic diseases. As the age of the population increases owing to the lowered birth rate and the prolongation of life, more people live to become demented, more people outlive their brains. Then too, as people become urbanized, it becomes more difficult to care for their demented elders in apartment houses and tenements; so instead of caring for them at home, they pack them off to institutions.

All in all, the rate of mental disease is not increasing. The fact that there are more institutions and that more money is being spent for them does not argue an increase in mental disease any more than spending more money for schools shows an increase in illiteracy. On the contrary, it demonstrates that the community is paying more attention to education. So, too, the building of hospitals and the increased cost of caring for the mentally sick mean a more humane attitude toward mental disease and, perhaps more importantly, a realistic social effort to understand and to cure it.

If we turn our attention to the inheritance of *feeblemindedness*, we are confronted at once by the studies of the ardent eugenists. In order to frighten the normal members of the community into stern and sterilizing action against the low-grade people of the community, these pointers-with-alarm have created a propaganda that is selective and biased. It assumes what it wishes whenever there are no facts. It takes exceptional cases and makes them typical. It neglects a whole world of contradictory statistics and facts.

The creation of the royal families of the feebleminded, the Nams, the Kallikaks, the Jukes, the tribes of Ishmael, the Virginians, and so on, is based on these serious errors of research. The typical technique is represented by the history of the Kallikaks. According to the legend, a certain Martin Kallikak, a Revolutionary soldier, had a liaison *sub rosa* with a "nameless feebleminded girl" whom he met in a tavern. All the descendants of the Martin Kallikak union with this anonymous moron were "studied," so the story goes, for four generations, and, lo and behold, they were all monsters; there were no normal people among them! All were alcoholics, feebleminded, criminals, or vagrants. This family is in sharp contrast to that which followed the union of Martin Kallikak's germ plasm with that of a presumably good girl. All the descendants of this public and approved union were fine, upstanding people — doctors, lawyers, judges, business men of repute. None of them were villains, shiftless alcoholics, insane, or feebleminded.

Since such a partition of germ-plasmic fate has never occurred in this world or the next, we have the right to raise two pertinent questions about this study. First, we might ask for assurance that Martin Kallikak actually fathered the child of the nameless feebleminded girl. And then, since it is often difficult even for the experienced psychiatrist to diagnose feeblemindedness in a patient he *sees*, we might question the mental disability of this Revolutionary maid. Unless these two basic queries can be answered with facts, the entire study of the Kallikaks is completely without value.

We find that all our information about the nameless girl and her child comes from an elderly lady who was questioned in 1910. This informant said that she had personally known the girl. If the feebleminded girl was born in 1760 and reached the age of eighty and the informant was eighty years of age in 1910, the paths of these two people would have crossed between 1830 and 1840, at which time the heroine of the Kallikak saga was seventy to eighty years of age and our informant was something under ten. Any other ages would make the thing entirely impossible. And so we are asked to believe that a woman of eighty in 1910 could recall from her childhood authentic information of scientific value about a person whose mental state is alleged to have profoundly influenced four generations of descendants.

No scientific study of any family of feebleminded people reveals a one-hundred-per-cent set of failures. Studies such as one we did in Massachusetts reveal no counterparts to the Kallikaks. In many groups we found feeblemindedness for one or two generations, but we also found collaterals who reached distinction and were respected in the community. On the other hand, we found no family tree, however distinguished, which did not have hanging from its branches the mentally sick, the defective, the alcoholic, the failure, the ne'er-do-well, and the social misfit.

What often is mistaken for feeblemindedness is low cultural level. Groups sequestered in the hills of Kentucky or in lonely sections of New Hampshire and Vermont breed low-grade people generation after generation, just as peasant communities throughout Europe are illiterate, superstitious, and low-grade. The cultural milieu is low-grade, and the social factors are so important that it is impossible to call this germ-plasm heredity rather than cultural. This dependence of mental development on cultural level has been well shown by the study that Freeman and his associates made of foster children moved from a low-grade environment to a better one. They found, for instance, that children who were tested before they were placed in foster homes, and then retested several years later, showed great improvement in their intelligence ratings, and also that the children in the better foster homes gained considerably more than those in the poorer ones.

When we regard the facts about feeblemindedness, we find that there are various types that are radically different biologically. Mongolian idiocy is certainly not related to feeblemindedness in general and arises in perfectly normal families. Cretinism is definitely a thyroid disturbance and may have some hereditary basis, but more likely is due either to spontaneous defect in the development of the thyroid gland or to the amount of iodine present in the drinking water and plants of the locality, as in Switzerland. A third type of feeblemindedness is due to injury at birth, when the brain is damaged because the head of the child is too large for the mother's pelvis.

It may, nevertheless, be stated that most feeblemindedness is related in some way to heredity. The concordance of identical twins is almost one hundred per cent. This heredity, however, need not be a direct one. A great

deal of feeblemindedness arises by some unknown hereditary combination in what appear to be normal families,
and, in fact, a study done by Popenoe, himself one of the
leading eugenists, shows that *the majority of the feebleminded in California had about the same kind of ances-
try as the normal population, so that there was no real
evidence of huge groups breeding feeblemindedness generation after generation.*

This brings us at once to a collateral question of great
importance. The statement is continually made that the
feebleminded breed much faster than do the normal members of the population, and the pointers-with-alarm cite
this as evidence of a deterioration of the race that is going
on apace and will end in feebleminded human species.
The investigations carried out by the British Royal Com-
mission appointed for this purpose completely contradict
this statement. The report says: "Except for a relatively
small number of isolated instances, we find that there is
no evidence of excessive fertility, and indeed it would be
easy to set off against these exceptional cases a much
larger number of cases in which the fertility rate was
low. The supposed abnormal fertility of defectives is, in
our view, largely mythical."

The birth rate of the feebleminded is no greater than
that of the population as a whole, and their mortality is
much higher, as is the mortality of all mentally sick people. Moreover, the marriage rate of the defective individuals is much less than that of the normal population.
This would naturally be the case. They are not so attractive. They find a greater difficulty in earning a living.
They have less sexual drive or, at any rate, a less normal

sexual drive. They tend to be isolated early by the very nature of their illness, and every social factor operates against their reproduction.

Now we come to epilepsy, which has been described from the earliest days of medicine and has been glorified as the sacred disease. Epilepsy is found throughout the whole mammalian kingdom, appears spontaneously in cats, dogs, and guinea pigs as well as man, and can be experimentally produced in practically all animals by the use of drugs.

Nevertheless, the disease remained of almost unknown pathology and cause until a fertile era of experimentation culminated in the marvelous discovery of the brain waves. It was learned that throughout life the brain as an electric organ gives off waves that can be captured, enormously magnified, and recorded on smoked paper. Then came the application of this discovery to the study of epilepsy. A group of notable Boston investigators demonstrated that in epilepsy disordered brain waves of specific types almost constantly appeared, even when the individual was ostensibly well. Drs. William Gordon Lennox, E. L. Gibbs, and F. A. Gibbs found that the brain waves of the parents, brothers, and sisters of the epileptic patient, even though these relatives themselves showed no evidence of epilepsy, had waves of the epileptic type in a very much larger proportion than those of the normal population. This demonstrates that there is a constitutional predisposition to epilepsy in the family group and gives an important clue to the heredity of this disease. Yet it is too early to say that this demonstrates a true heredity. The fact that epilepsy can be reproduced experimentally and that definite environmental agents, such as illness and brain injury, create the disease in otherwise healthy individuals and in animals leads to the conclusion that, in addition to the hereditary factor, some unknown environmental agent co-operates to bring about the actual epileptic attacks.

It is not at all true that the epileptic is necessarily an inferior person. Epilepsy is a very widespread disorder occurring sporadically among all people, regardless of their social status or intelligence. When the attacks are very frequent, mental deterioration takes place as a secondary factor; that is, it is caused by the effects of attacks and the drugs used to control them. Fortunately, there has been great improvement in the treatment of this condition. Drugs now used exercise a very beneficial effect without so much narcosis as was necessary in the past. Further work promises exceedingly well for the future, and undoubtedly the time will come when the epileptic attack will be a rarity.

A book might be devoted to the question of criminality. I do not believe that criminality is a mental disease. Crime is socially defined, and each society has its own criteria of what constitutes crime. Thus, it was a crime to be a Jew in Nazi Germany. The leading crime of the Middle Ages was heresy; in times of war it is a crime not to believe what the majority believes about the enemy. The banker, who is now the touchstone of respectability, was a criminal in the days when it was declared immoral to receive interest on loans. In the United States selling liquor was a crime during the prohibition era, but now, because of a few turns in the wheel of legal definition, it is again a respectable business. While it was proper to have many wives during the days of my distant ancestor Abraham, in my day this would constitute polygamy and be punishable by incarceration. The whole sorry history of what man has done in making laws to which others were compelled to conform destroys any belief that the law-breaker is necessarily abnormal.

Statistics showing that members of the same families become criminals do not take into account the fact that members of the same families usually have the same general social background as well. There *are* abnormal characters who come in contact with the law, who become declared criminals. There are just as many, perhaps more, abnormal characters who are zealous defenders of the law and who uphold it with great firmness. I think I have seen as many psychopathic judges, lawyers, police officers, and psychiatrists as psychopathic criminals.

To believe that the laws men make have some internal relationship to an absolute morality is to disregard completely the whole history of human belief and credulity. Thus, the laws about sex are being violated everywhere. Punishment is given only for the perversions of sex and in relation to the social status of the offender. The poor and unfortunate girl who gets into sexual difficulties comes to the attention of society. The delinquencies of her high-placed sister are treated by a surprisingly efficient method of "hush-hush." The poor boy who steals or commits assault and battery lands in a reform school and is thus committed to a dynamicism of serious trouble.

The well-to-do boy who shows these tendencies is rescued from the law by the power of money and position and has time to organize himself.

The best geneticists are definitely wary of including crime as a hereditary matter. Herbert Spencer Jennings quite eloquently states that the genetic approach to crime is not at the present time of any practical importance and stresses education, training, better health conditions, and better economic circumstances as the fruitful measures by which criminality could be lessened. Lesser folk, ardent to rescue man from all kinds of difficulty, would sterilize the criminal. But a very much safer attitude is expressed by the sentimental utterance: "There but for the grace of God go I." Fortunately for most of us, the time, the place, and the opportunity do not frequently coincide with our illegal and criminalistic desires.

When we consider sterilization for schizophrenia, the manic-depressive psychoses, feeblemindedness, and epilepsy, the four conditions for which it is most widely urged, we find that our present knowledge does not warrant compulsory sterilization of all who suffer from these conditions. Nevertheless, it seems to me that there is sufficient evidence on hand to legitimatize the sterilization of carefully selected cases, in each case taking into account the assets as well as the liabilities that the individual could transmit to his descendants.

Some years ago I was the chairman of a committee that surveyed this question and arrived at some moderate conclusions. We favored sterilization for selected cases and believed that it should be voluntary — that is, performed with the consent of the patient or of those responsible for him. Seeing no reason for group or class discrimination, we decided that it should be applicable not only to patients in state institutions but also to those in private institutions and those at large in the community. We felt that the essential machinery for administering such a law should be one or several boards composed chiefly of persons who have had special training and experience in the problems involved and who could evaluate each case on its individual merits. Cases could be brought before such a board by superintendents of institutions, private physicians, parents or guardians or by the patients themselves. This arrangement would promote elasticity in the application of the law, and permit the utilization of future advances in knowledge.

We felt no hesitation in recommending sterilization in the case of feeblemindedness. Though we hesitated to stress any purely social necessity for sterilization, it is obvious that in the case of the feebleminded there may be a social as well as a biological situation of importance. Since most of the feebleminded can hardly care for themselves, a family of children may prove an overwhelming burden.

We believed that schizophrenia would need relatively little attention from the surgeon because most cases that are recognized in time to prevent procreation spend their days in hospitals anyway. Moreover, the sexual urge and the marriage and birth rate are low. Sterilization might well be recommended, however, for those patients living in the community, since desirable qualities of other kinds are only incidental to schizophrenia and not part of its make-up.

As for the manic-depressive psychoses, there are problems that would tax the judgment of the wisest board and that must be met with conservatism and caution. The manic-depressive temperament is frequently associated with the highest achievement and ability of which mankind can boast. In this disease particularly, the decision would have to take into account the total assets of the individual character as well as the liabilities incident to the psychosis.

As for epilepsy, we believed that if the individual's epileptic attacks were infrequent and if the qualities of the personality were intact, there was no reason for recommending sterilization.

In the past, marriage has acted as a selective agency operating in a eugenic way. When there was little efficient treatment for schizophrenia, the malignant manic-depressive state, and severe epilepsy, the commitment rate and the patients' obvious mental condition kept down their marriage and birth rates. But we are entering an era when the schizophrenic will be improved, the depressive states sharply curtailed without hospital stay, and the fits of the epileptic will be either greatly reduced or entirely prevented. We shall make them more marriageable and more socially efficient, therefore more likely to have offspring. Still, there is no danger that the race will go to the dogs, and we do not have to accept any measures born of panic or of dogma, unjustified by sure facts.

A long-term, carefully carried-out research program is the first essential for understanding not only the heredity but the nature of the major inheritable mental conditions.

The life span of any investigator is short, and he may not exceed the years of his subject, the patient. So intricate is the net of human relationships and kinship, so little does anyone really know about his own kin, that to draw conclusions from the studies that have appeared in the field of eugenics and psychiatry is to state that ten times zero equals something. Vagueness added to vagueness, surmise piled upon surmise, do not build the edifice of science. When we shall really study human families carefully and systematically for at least a hundred years, so that we can view three generations in the clear light of well-established facts and records, then we shall have some knowledge of the relationship of heredity to eminence and genius, as well as to mental disease and social difficulty.

Even though we may believe that a condition is hereditary, we must not dismiss the environmental influences as nonrelevant. We have been mistaken before. Moreover, the dependence of the expression of hereditary qualities upon an evocative environment is the most important single thing we know about the occurrence of hereditary qualities. In our environment there may be evocative factors — social, traditional, cultural, as well as physical — that bring about the inheritance of schizophrenia, manic-depressive state, epilepsy, and possibly, although this is not likely, feeblemindedness.

It is the duty of any reasonable society to know about the constitution of its members. No such effort has been made even in the most advanced commonwealths. A long-time survey of the potentialities of the members of our society is necessary for a proper, reasonable organization. Every time we go to war and examine the potential fighting members of the group, we are surprised at the amount of defect. No such surprise is warranted. The surprise is that there is not more defect. Man uses his intelligence less in the care of his own species than he does in his care of anything else he owns or governs. It is a cardinal article of faith with me that it would be good eugenics, as well as good euthenics to wipe out every slum, to secure for everyone access to sunshine and good food, cultural opportunities, and those things which stimulate the growth of intelligence; to eliminate the infectious diseases and especially those diseases such as syphilis and tuberculosis which may injure more than one generation. A large part of our population, even in the best of our commonwealths, live in circumstances in which we would expect deterioration in plants and animals. At any rate, we can say that while a limited eugenic program is warranted at this time, even more important would be a radical improvement in the environment of civilized man and an organized research into the nature of those mental conditions from which he suffers, so that we can work with understanding and intelligence.

CHAPTER XIII

DESIRE AND MENTAL HEALTH

I⸢T⸣ is difficult for an old and sick man to write with
full pungency of desire and satisfaction. But being old,
even being sick, does not necessarily involve all of a man,
since from birth to death we are a mosaic of qualities
rather than a unified pattern. Thus my hair was old
when I was twenty-five but my teeth, derived from the
same ectodermic layer, are young at sixty-six. My interest in life is as keen as ever; I cannot talk without enthusiasm of science or of psychiatric problems; and I find
a deep though painful joy in a beautiful day. I can thrill
with delight and love just to be with my grandchildren,
and the one I love most in this world still looks sweet and
inexpressibly dear to me.

I find myself hot with indignation (in a way that is
bad for my heart) when I reflect on the state of the
world, on the hypocrisy and lies that are the main mani-
festations of international relationship, and on the brutality and cynicism in high places. I despair (but with
sardonic humor) when I reflect on the *interest and admiration level* of the populace, since in these most critical
days a thousand times more Americans are concerned
with baseball than with the functioning of the UN, and
Ted Williams is admired far more than Dr. Fleming. (To
ease the reader's mind, Dr. Alexander Fleming discov-

ered penicillin.) When one can feel, as I do, that life is worth living merely to live it, merely to rejoice in strength and beauty, merely to work at whatever advances or seems to advance science, art, and human well-being without any absolute or certainty of goal, then one can write adequately of seeking and finding.

Haeckel, the great naturalist, asked a terrible question that reflective men, seeking serenity, have tried to answer. He asked: "Is the universe friendly?" I do not believe the question can be answered except by faith, which, alas, is the more powerful the less one knows about the universe. This leaves the attitude of the universe direfully unknown to me. While I have seen no evidence that man is more important than a microbe, I do state — and at a time when the commonplace "All men must die" suddenly becomes charged with meaning — that life has valid subjective values. These values depend on the normalcy of desire and satisfaction.

I find this subject especially interesting because in the past forty years I have seen so many thousands of patients lacking the vigorous desire that is the essence of fundamental mental health. The captious critic who resides within me tries to crush me by saying, "All psychiatrists make the same mistake — they try to reconstruct the world in the image of their pathological experience. All division is *not* schizophrenia; all sadness is *not* manic-depressive psychosis; all obsession (and anxiety) is *not* neurosis, just as every pain in the belly is not appendicitis."

True enough, my alter ego; just what I was going to say, with this modifying addendum: physiology has had one of its roots in pathology, because normal function is often too swift to analyze, and disease isolates factors and their function. So we, as doctors, have constructed the normal from the hints and clues of disease. The proud knowledge of the function of the internal glands, for example, stems from disease, since the abnormalities of thyroid secretion dramatically and extravagantly tell us that the gland secretes a substance which in excess drives the human being into a pulsating, sweating, eye-bulging, heart-racing case of hyperthyroidism, or in absence may reduce him to a fat, baldish, inert mass of dementia. Guided by these extremes, the scientist goes on to place the thyroid gland in the brilliantly evolved human ecology of glands and their chemistry.

I am sure it was the accidental or congenital eunuch whose affliction led men to the discovery of the castrate, so that oxen could plow fields, the Oriental tyrant could create dispassionate guardians of harems, and, during the Renaissance, neuter-gender sopranos could sing in Christian churches. All this finally led to knowledge of paternity, masculinity, fertilization, and heredity. Accident, illness, and the curious deviations from normal that spring from impartial Nature's laboratories have slowed down the whirring wheels of living action so that the spokes can be seen. Men have seized upon the abnormal as a basis for that experimentation and study which leads to the knowledge of the normal.

In short, and to answer myself, because on countless occasions I have seen the total impairment of desire and satisfaction, I have concluded that the importance of understanding the laws of healthy desire and satisfaction equals that of any other knowledge we may have, and that its immediate and practical importance is greater than that of any other study we can make. Let those who will, study the relation of man to God, of this life to another one; I will not quarrel with them. Let those who can, build up the knowledge of mathematics, physics, chemistry, biology, and sociology so that we shall have a background for studies of human desire and satisfaction.

Without being too fine about the matter, let us say that melancholia is anhedonia — that is, the very opposite of desire or hedonism. Now, it must be made clear that desire in the sense of pleasure-seeking is not the primary principle, that there is a behavior antecedent to pleasure and entirely unconscious. The beetle, which prepares food for young that it never sees, the salmon, whose spawning activities involve incredible effort and almost complete wasting and death, are not presumably seeking anything that we can call pleasure. With them racial instincts very definitely seem paramount. Moreover, we cannot conceive that the creatures which go through the turmoil of sex, mating, nursing, and care of the young visualize or understand the goals of their activity, and, in fact, only in relatively recent times have human beings known what the sexual antics meant in relationship to the baby born nine months later. Curiously enough, one of the difficulties of our time is that sexual union has become charged with intense personal motivations which, to a great extent, deny the racial purpose.

So desire need not have happiness or well-being as a goal except as it in some way brings about the discharge of an unpleasant tension. The "desire" for defecation or urination brings a relief from discomfort in itself pleasurable, and it may be argued that sexual tension is discharged so that relief rather than satisfaction is the goal. There is, of course, the school of thought from the Hindu ascetics down to Freud which says that all desire is painful and that we seek not joy or pleasure but relief from pain and discomfort. This is a dismal doctrine, and it would seem as if its exponents had never experienced ecstasy. Yet it is, at least in part, true.

There is a group of mental sicknesses characterized by an absence or severe impairment of desire and satisfaction. Whether or not the patient can sleep (and he usually sleeps poorly), whether or not he loses weight, or whatever mental symptoms are present, the appetites for all kinds of doing are absent, and recovery is the return of desiring. In the lesser cases there is the desire *to desire* — oh, such a yearning for it, though in a blind sort of way; but in the extreme states the patient loses even the yearning to yearn. This disease affects all forms of appetite. The epicure and the glutton, as well as those whose normal food drive is reasonable, lose their desire to eat. When recovery takes place (say because of a few electric shocks), the glutton goes back to his gluttony, the epicure to his finickiness, and the normal eater to his way of life. Mental health in this respect is not the restoration of what we call good or normal habits, but the return of strong desire and adequate satisfaction. In this disease sexual desire also is lost. The masturbator ceases masturbating, the homosexual becomes moral, the adulterer gives up adultery, and the man with focalized, socially approved sexual feeling ceases to desire his wife. Sexual desire, whatever its goal, disappears and the tendency to explain sexual pathology disappears as well. There is no drive for reform, though when health returns, normality again floats morality.

One of the most incorrigible of the drives of man is to gamble, to seek fortune on a throw of the dice, the shuffle of cards, the fleetness of a horse's hoof — in short, passionately to woo Lady Luck in her countless seductive forms. The mood that destroys the validity of any and all the drives makes of Lady Luck a "snotty-nosed baggage," in the words of one gambler, whose reform was complete until a formula of treatment, which cured his depression, gave to wanton Fortune all of her old allure. We also find that many heavy drinkers give up drinking when melancholy, because they no longer enjoy company and get no satisfaction from alcohol.

It is not a case of "the Devil was sick, the Devil a monk would be; the Devil was well, the devil a monk was he," for I have heard the industrious repent of their industry, the strait-laced of their inhibitions, when sick. The object of desire may be socially or morally good, bad, or indifferent, but so long as there is no desire, the individual is not well.

Just as surely as the "immoral" become moral, so do the pious lose their appetite for church devotion and good deeds. Altruism tends to disappear just as much as, perhaps more than, egoism. The natural love and interest in one's children goes and, in fact, an irritability, even hate, replaces all directions of love. To the normal man life is made up of interest in little things. Conversation, derision and gossip, the choice of a necktie, who won the baseball game, the baby's first step, two children running a race, the stranger who rang the bell at the neighbor's house when the male neighbor was away and the female was alone — these may be the small change of living, but only a few live with the thousand-dollar bill as their currency. As interest turns inward, this outward interest disappears or is with difficulty aroused, and what remains is continued introspection, a nightmare of gloom. And, of course, the daily work, even if it is not fundamentally exciting, has for the normal man an interest and an absorption that are lost with the advent of melancholy. Most human beings love to meet and talk with others, yet even the great primary drive of gregariousness may completely disappear when the mood is lowered into anhedonia. Thus the sociable become timid or hostile and find that conversation bores, irritates, or seems like the idle chatter of unreal puppets.

What seems to be clear is that ardor, with consequent satisfaction and interest, has a general background independent of morals, social validity, and the goals of the person; it disappears when melancholy appears on the scene, and reappears with the return of normal mood. This ardor, I believe, is due to factors of energy and recuperation. These factors are injured not only by mental illness but also by such "normal" conditions as fatigue or old age.

As we go along from youth to old age, the appetites of life diminish, and the requirements for satisfaction increase. So we remember the thrill of that first *Hamlet* we saw as a boy of seventeen, and we remember that the last one, at fifty-seven, gave no such ecstasy. But neither did anything else in that fifty-seventh year give the naïve joy of that wonderful period when the juices of life could be set astreaming at a look or a touch, and when an embrace was an immersion in complete self-forgetfulness. In later years the law of diminishing returns takes a heavy toll of present joys, and the law of myth-formation extols the past in comparison. In any controversy as to whether Caruso and the singers of "old" were better singers than those of the present day, all the older people insist on the superiority of the former stars. Elderly sport fans are quite certain that John L. Sullivan could lick half the present crop of heavyweights with one hand and practically at one blow. Such comparisons of the past with the present are always influenced by the age of the comparer.

A lowered threshold of desire can also be caused by refinement. Refinement builds up the æsthetics and the beauty of life, but carried too far, made too important, it balances the pyramid of desire on its apex and increases the liability to unsatisfaction and disgust. Our appetites are injured by our efforts to cover up the animal, to disguise and refine viscerality. We dine in approved manner, so that eating and devouring are gilded over by refinement and beauty. We get married by ceremonies that now only hint at the primitive notions which underlie our ideas of sexual union. We squelch extra gusto and the harsh vigor of desire. We put brakes on the animal expression of emotion, so that even the grief-stricken have pocket handkerchiefs ready to disguise the mucous fluidity of eyes and nose.

Much of our humor mocks that phase of refinement

which conceals the organic and visceral. In the Moham-
medan culture, my father said, it was an unpardonable
breach of manners to break wind. It happened that one
Hassam ben Adam, on his way to be married, involun-
tarily expressed his nervousness by breaking wind. Flee-
ing from the horrified wedding guests, he went to a distant land, took up a new life, and gathered together the
shattered remnants of his egotism. Twenty years later,
obsessed with a yearning for his native land, he disguised
himself in every possible way and revisited his former
haunts. In a café he heard a man discussing a famous
murder. "When did all this happen?" asked a second
man. "Oh," said the first, "don't you remember? It occurred in the year when Hassam ben Adam broke wind."
Poor Hassam fled again.

Our efforts to disguise the animal within are more or
less futile. We are born as animals, and so we remain.
Eventually we learn that even the idealized, deanimalized
woman of our dreams has bowel and bladder functions
and monthly catamenia. The processes of digestion, copulation, defecation, urination, sweating, getting old, and
dying remain primitive. So a psychological division, a
social ambivalence, takes place between gusto and refinement. This is a critical inner struggle of man, because,
as I have said, heartiness of appetite is the basis of
health, mental and physical, and whatever injures desire
and satisfaction leads to illness and melancholy.

The hearty, primitive appetite starts from a primal
need and thus takes what we call "natural" directions.
As man becomes conscious of his desires and his satisfactions, he seeks refinement and ceremony. This may

be called the stage of civilization and is an expression of the great artistry of man and of his self-manipulation. As consciousness of desire and satisfaction becomes over-developed, the primitiveness of appetite declines and so-phistication enters the scene. The primitive natural reactions and attitudes become more or less despised as animal-like or common. According to Vaihinger's principle, the means tend to become more important than the ends they originally served.

The aim of eating, for example, is to ingest sufficient food to maintain health and vigor. The original means, which lead to the end, eating, are the obtaining of the materials. It took a long time for man to evolve cooking, and, up to what might be called yesterday, his only table instrument was a knife.

I once saw a movie that showed King Richard the Lion-Hearted at dinner. The King was seated on a rude stool before a rude table, and near him was a great dog. Before the King was a large pot into which he thrust his kingly paw, fished around for what he wanted, divided it, threw a bit to the dog, and put the rest into the kingly maw. Dog and man ate with about the same ceremony and with equal gusto. It is difficult to believe that King Richard the Lion-Hearted might have become disgusted with service or upset over the trifles of dining.

As a counterfoil, let us imagine some kingly descendant of Richard eating in the palace at Westminster. The large table is covered with snowy linen, an endless procession of dishes is brought in by liveried servitors, and there are so many instruments for the proper serial ingestion of the food that it becomes quite a feat to wind up the meal with the right knife or fork and nothing left over. A spot of gravy on the tablecloth, a dish not sufficiently clean, or something served out of its proper order might well take away the kingly zest by producing disgust and thus destroying appetite, the prime requisite for successful eating.

The means of dining have become overceremonialized and almost as important as the end — that is, to eat. I have been at a table where a young child was feeding himself and have watched the vigor of his appetite badgered into destruction by his mother's endeavor to instill manners and refinement. "Break your bread . . . don't suck your spoon . . . don't make so much noise . . . don't lick your plate. . . ." The means, becoming overintensified, interfere with heartiness and appetite. Nothing is good unless there is a good appetite for it; and where means become too important, satisfaction becomes too nicely poised, and consequently disgust may the more disturb appetite.

This thesis becomes immensely important and fascinating as we examine the sexual habits and attitudes of man. Thus courtship is a means and should be, relatively speaking, a short preparation for the sexual union. As manifested in bewildering and diversified ways, it becomes almost an end and sometimes an endless end. The forepleasures of kissing and embracing, which again are preparatory means, become conventionalized and staticized into the all-in-all of a relationship between men and women. Creating tensions without relief and a preparedness for action that never eventuates, they build up false expectation and indeed lessen virility and the ecstasy of the sexual act itself. The quarrel between the social customs of man and his cruder biological nature get their most striking examples in this colorful and ever interesting zone of life.

Perhaps the most recent development, and one that is changing the whole age distribution of the human species, is birth-control. I have no quarrel with birth-control and believe that man must take steps against ruthless propagation and that very likely, in the long run, more good than harm comes from birth-control. The time will undoubtedly come when some injection or series of injections will sterilize a woman for a time, so that the sexual act can take place naturally and without too much technique. At present its techniques are crude and, putting a strain on the sexual relationship, often lead to dissatisfaction and fatigue. A formidable preparation subtracts the ecstasy from love-making.

We find a different route to the death of desire in the individual who develops a sensualism so gross that he loses all restraint and gives himself over to uninhibited excess. From this he may go on to a complete loss of normal desire and a fevered seeking of the bizarre, the unusual, and the exotic so as to gain a satisfaction otherwise difficult to obtain. But whatever form the sensualism takes, whether it be gluttony or sexual excess, the lustfulness itself breeds ennui, so that the final result is a mental-physical nausea.

A good deal of human history has been written by those individuals who, because of revulsion based on knowledge of the abnormal, or natural anhedonia, or loss of their own sexual potency, renounced desire and satisfaction. These people have declared that the flesh is vile, desire an illusion, satisfaction vain and impossible; that there must be renunciation of that sensuality which leads only to dust and ashes. Through their great eloquence and influence they have created grave inner turmoil among their normal followers. Consequently there comes into life that strange renunciation and denunciation which is called asceticism.

Asceticism is the specialty of man. We know of no other creature that could consider itself vile, its body obscene, and its vital functions offensive. If we ask ourselves how such fantastic notions could arise, we may get an answer by a brief study of the chief locus of asceticism, in both ancient and modern times.

Ideas grow into social practices wherever the social soil is favorable, just as the apple tree flourishes in the Northern United States and not in the jungle. The denial of the flesh has its most consistent advocates and followers — where? In India, a country where the flesh is flaunted by the heartless magnificence of the rich, where gods and goddesses with many breasts and many phalluses exhibit sexual orgy at its height and are worshipped by the bulk of the population. This is the land where abject misery, famine, and wars are so prevalent that they seem as natural as the contours of the great subcontinent itself; where the shocking and fantastically rigid caste system makes the lot of most human beings worse than that of dogs; and where the withdrawal of a little group of foreigners let loose the most savage massacres of modern history. The notion that Indians are generally ascetics, devoted to other-worldliness and non-striving is romantic nonsense. Nirvana is the philosophy of an insignificant minority whose professional asceticism and renunciation are in sharp contrast to the prevailing sensuality, sloth, disease, cruelty, and barbaric idol-worship. The senseless, degraded untouchables and the strutting rajah are nearer the real India than Buddha or Mahatma Gandhi.

Sensualism and asceticism are natural and associated polarities, and it is ironically true that sensualism breeds its foe and rival. For the reflective man such as Buddha, the evils of life and the foreknowledge of death and old age make all effort and striving seem meaningless. These disgusted folk tend to throw out the baby with the dirty bath water. Disgust, fatigue, and impassioned revolt lead to the throwing out of the baby, the legitimate desire, and finally all human craving and pleasure, with the evils of excess. Since sex leads to profligacy, out with sex. Since eating with heartiness leads to gluttony, down with eating. Because ambition and striving lead to war, cruelty, cheating, lies, avaunt all effort and striving. Because artistic living is the road to exhibitionism and vanity, down with art. I believe that while "throwing out the baby with the dirty water" is an old saying, its full wisdom has never been fully appreciated, and that it is a real law of human life.

The ascetic, who renounces the world, the flesh, and the Devil, who dwells in the desert and wears a hair shirt, who never bathes, who munches dried peas and drinks rain water, is by no means anhedonic. Though the ascetic renounces the desires of the flesh, he, like St. Anthony, is tormented by them. The savage attack on

woman by the ascetics of all times is the outward manifestation of the torment she creates in the continent, as if
she were to blame for the vain desire she evokes. In a
sense, the ascetic by damning certain of his desires has
canalized his drives into a fierce yearning for heaven, for
God's approval, for that of the censor within him, for
the satisfaction of being able to withstand temptation,
for the glory of being a sort of moral athlete who can
demonstrate how resistant and powerful he is. In many
lands and in many times down to our own the ascetic
has been a professional, has belonged to organized
groups, and has even made his living, such as it was, by
asceticism.

I believe that the capacity to desire, to enjoy, and to
be satisfied are in large measure as innate as the shape of
one's nose; that there are people born to be hearty regardless of life's buffets, and others who are so constituted
that they pass through the world zestless and ready for
melancholy. William James said there are some who are
born with an eternal bottle of champagne to their credit.
I would add to this that there are others who enter life
with a chloroform sponge under their noses. Some in-
fants thrive on whatever they eat and take with gusto
whatever is offered them. Others from the first turn away
from food and drive their parents wild because of lack
of appetite — an amazing state of affairs, since hunger
for food is the basis of survival. While the hearty child
may become finicky and the zestless one become hearty,
I do not believe that this is the rule, although it would
be difficult to prove the statement.

What is true of the innate nature of the appetite and

desire for food is, I believe, true of the sexual drive, the zest for sociality, the craving and ambition for success and status. There are those whose life centers on sex, its triumphs, its struggles, and its sensualities; and there are eunuchs by temperament, although they seem well endowed with the organs of copulation and reproduction, who wonder why people are "so crazy about intercourse." Just as some people never have a real hunger for food and therefore eat mainly through custom and necessity, others lack sexual appetite almost entirely. These are the cold and frigid types, who, as they see themselves in contrast with others, become alarmed and anxious over their defect and sometimes seek to stimulate themselves into sexual activity, but who fail since desire is finally the root of all successful conduct. These people can, and often do, remain virginal, continent, and so live what seem to others unfulfilled lives. If they happen to be women, they marry without any feeling or knowledge of what sex really is and are appalled by it or yield frigidly to the demands of their mates. The frigid woman, the impotent man, both enter prominently into the scope of the daily work of the psychiatrist, and their defect may come because sickness has entered upon the scene to destroy a previous normal appetite and power. In the depressive states and in many of the neuroses the sexual life becomes impaired or difficult and creates conflicts within the individual as well as within his home. This impairment does not, I believe, in the majority of instances cause the depression or the neurosis, but is part of the expression of melancholy and nervous fatigue.

The appetite for sex is like that for food — if one is really hungry, a ham sandwich is divine; if one is nauseated, the finest table only increases the nausea. I believe there is a vast innate range of desire, which may embrace all the desires or include this one and that one haphazardly. The man with a hearty appetite for food may be a cold fish as far as women are concerned.

I agree that the word "appetite" may be too simple, "desire" too narrow, and "drive" misleading, but I say that the healthy life from the mental standpoint lies not so much in the goal as in the ardor. In part there are certain rules and satisfactions. Thus so long as our friend the spinster social worker felt satisfaction in her work, so long as she woke up each morning eager to start the day, she was substantially well, even though her sex life was balked. So long as she slept well at night and awoke with energy, she was well — mentally. If she had friends and liked to meet with them, enjoyed the theater, could become absorbed in a book, she was well. If the inner turmoil could be dismissed as she worked, if she could face others without too shrinking a timidity, if she felt that she could shrug off her disappointments and disillusionment, she was well, even though the biological sexual urges found no satisfaction.

Unfortunately, I can offer no precepts and no suggestions for banishing melancholy or for arousing healthy desire. Even if injunctions are good on paper, they may be mere stale truisms that the social milieu and the personal circumstances render futile. I have often raged at the comfortable M.D. who tells his patient to work less, to relax, to go on a trip, to avoid worry, when all the circumstances of the poor devil are such that he must keep his nose to a whirring grindstone.

The good life cannot be put into any phrase, since, to begin with, one must have an appetite for living. The healthy appetite is the *sine qua non* of all human striving, effort, and seeking; satisfaction is a goal subjectively defined for each man. All one can say is that man seems to have made the going tough for the healthfulness of his desires and satisfaction.

CHAPTER XIV

MIND AND BODY

Primitive man divided himself into two main parts, body and spirit. Religion built the concept of spirit into theories of an immortal soul as something separable from and having, to some extent, an existence independent of the body. The body came to be despised as the source of sin. As the flesh became the synonym for evil and for weakness, this separation became more dogmatic and was elevated into a theological philosophy. When dogmatic religion weakened with the revival of learning and the quick advance of science, spirit disappeared from scientific discussions, and mind became its heir as something separate, something even immanent. Very great scientists declared that there was no way in which mental activities, especially consciousness, could be linked up with the molecular physical structure of the brain. Thus they fathered the parallelistic theory by which mind processes and brain processes ran side by side, parallel to each other, and, Euclidean-like, never meeting.

They were wrong. There is no mind without a body, though I have seen the reverse. In each human being, mind evolves with body. The mind is infantile when the body is, and it goes on to maturity of function and then retrogresses as the body does.

The infant is an unorganized bundle of activities without governing habits, skills, trends, or purposes. As he passes into childhood, organization becomes more dominant and conduct more social, although his emotions are still labile and violent. With adolescence come purpose, ambition, the daydream in which the goal is attained by a stroke of the imagination and lived in an ivory tower of fulfilled longing. With maturity, reality obtrudes itself, and the daydream, except in a few individuals, disappears or becomes less important. Now the intelligence is at its most evolved level and, except in pathological individuals, the mood tends to be fairly constant and the emotions are under better control. Then comes middle life. The height of life's evolution has been reached and the involution, physical and mental, starts in varying degree. The retrogressive processes begin to take their toll of physical disability and a lowering of mood, emotion, and energy. At the end comes old age, with the completion of these processes. If mind is memory, speech, abstract ideas, conceptual thinking, moral code, vigor of will and action, emotional state, conscience, affection, competitiveness, and altruism, it is very difficult to see how mind can be considered an entity separate from body.

As a physician I could show you many patients who have lost some or all of these functions because of the condition of their bodies. Let us stroll through the wards of a hospital for patients with nervous and mental disease. We shall see that independence of mind and body becomes the palest and most anemic theory when confronted with the facts of medicine, and especially neuropsychiatry.

Here is a patient who was once a very useful and

capable man, whose life on the whole was well regulated. He followed the conventions of moral conduct, was good-natured and kindly, was capable in his work, and showed normal instinctive and emotional responses, until the organism of syphilis, which had entered his body in his eighteenth year, began to produce well-known pathological changes in his brain. In short, this man developed the disease known as *general paresis*. Physically, he has a marked tremor, his reflex responses are increased, and fluid taken from his spinal column shows definite signs of inflammation of the brain.

When we study this man's mentality and personality, we find it radically changed, *pari passu*, with the disease of his brain. More explicitly, the living cells of his brain are sick, and their chemistry is altered. His memory is very bad. He lives from moment to moment. He has a foolish cheerfulness, and despite the fact that he is a poor devil in a hospital for mental diseases, he says he is a king, has millions of dollars, is the finest, the handsomest, and the brightest man in the world. He even may claim that he is God, ungodlike as he looks or acts. Whatever skills or learning he had are gone. His will and his purposes, his mood and emotions, his instincts and intelligence — in short, his personality — are markedly impaired.

Let us go further into sickness. Here is a patient who followed the usual pattern from infancy through middle life into old age, and now the arteries of his brain are diseased. The mind of this individual has become involved. His memory is very poor, and he lives in the past, hardly noticing or else misinterpreting the present

moment. He is petulant and irritable. To call him child-
ish would be a slur on the child, for this man lacks active
curiosity and lives in a sort of torpor, awaiting the final
coma. This is *senile dementia* — a typical example of the
dependence of the functions we call mind on bodily processes and structures.

Now let us examine a patient whose thyroid gland
has lowered its output of chemicals into the bloodstream.
As her metabolism lessened, she became very fat, her
hair became coarse and her skin dry. The personality and
mentality of this woman also were distorted. She is apa-
thetic, and her loss of energy has reduced her to a vege-
tative existence. Her instinctive drives have disappeared,
and neither sex, nor work, nor social relationship has
value and meaning. Her intelligence is only reminiscent
of what it once was, and her capacity to learn has disappeared. When this woman is treated with the thyroid
substance extracted from the glands of sheep and pigs,
who are certainly non-human but whose control of the
output of iodine can save the day, she will show a marked
change. As her thyroid level reaches normal, the extra
fat will disappear, the hair and face become normal
in structure and contour, the bodily heat increase, and
the personality re-emerge, perhaps not in the full
measure of its original power and drive, but vastly improved.

We pass along to a man who has used a chemical de-
vice for altering personality, for transforming mentality
and mood, for circumventing morality, convention, inhibition, and all that galls the rebellious flesh. For many
years he has imbibed too much alcohol, and he now

stands before us tremulous, agitated, and confused. He has visual and auditory hallucinations that convince him that he is in the midst of a fantastic and threatening world. In his mind past and present are so mingled that he is neither here nor there. When sober, he is equable, pleasant, skillful, and intelligent, weak only in his urge to excessive drinking. This urge periodically becomes a chain of inexorable binding links that wind tighter and tighter around him until a mental disease appears, as a result of which society confines him until, willy-nilly, sobriety returns.

Today we know that as he drinks he stops eating, and his diet becomes especially deficient in the various vitamins of the B complex. It is both this deficiency and the effect of the alcohol on his brain cells that are responsible for his psychosis. Those things which give individuality and personality, which mark the man, which evidence the intact mind, disappear or decrease, and the case of *delirium tremens* appears in our wards. If structures have not been too badly damaged, as the body re-establishes itself, repair takes place, reorganization appears, and the normal man emerges.

When the old woman appealed from Philip drunk, who had unjustly sentenced her, to Philip sober, she was exhorting two different men. Every time a man takes a drink to feel better or to lessen the sorrows of existence or to enter more harmoniously into the activities of a group, he proves the organic physico-chemical dependence of mind. He proves that mind is not an entity existing apart from the body. The philosopher can be as subtle and as dialectic as he pleases; he himself disproves his thesis when his blood alcohol level rises beyond 0.05 milligrams per cent.

Finally, we see a war veteran who unfortunately stopped a bullet with his genitals, as heroic as stopping it with his chest, but productive of curiously disgusting results. The personality shifts that took place and landed him in a hospital had their outward replica in his hairless face, his falsetto voice, his enlarged breasts and softened fat-infiltrated skin. This man had been transformed into a feminized eunuch, and the shrapnel that burst into his life tore apart in equal measure his testes and his place in the world.

For centuries man has recognized this particular dependence of mind on body and has transformed the personality of his domestic animals by eunuchizing them. While the bull is the symbol of ferocious male vigor, the ox, merely the bull minus his testes, is the symbol of passive slavery. And the polygamous lord used as guards for his harem mutilated males whose personality was as different as their structures were minus.

The individual's sexual response is directly dependent on certain conditions of his body. It is, for instance, very obviously dependent on his age. While the infant shows outward physical differentiation of sex, the sexual glands have not yet started to produce their particular products, and modern study of the hormones clearly shows that the infant is only latently sexual. This is important in view of Freud's theory that the sexuality of the infant is a dominant drive in its life. However ingenious this theory may be, it is merely a conversion of the infant's obvious sensuality into sexuality and does not harmonize with what we know of the infant biologically. In later childhood, while sexual feeling is rudimentary, sexual divergence is commencing to appear. There is not only a latent difference in the psychological attitudes of boy and girl, but also different environmental pressures acting on each sex.

With adolescence, boy becomes sexual male and girl becomes sexual female, their every attitude colored by the rich hues of sex with its concomitant difficulties, its broodings, and its longings, as well as its overt drives toward sexual relationships.

With maturity, sexual differentiation is taken for granted. In the woman we find that each monthly shift of the hormonic balance influences her personality and governs her sexual desire. In the man we find that his sexual desire mounts when his seminal vesicles are tense with sperms, that then he will avidly seek a mate. When his desire is satisfied, the mate who has satisfied it may even arouse dislike and disgust. One of the most important, and least expressed, of the phenomena of life is post-coital disgust, and the true historian of morals would give this phenomenon a great place in the evolution of the moral code. When, in the story of *Sapho*, the hero carries the seductive woman up several flights of stairs before he achieves what he yearns for, and then afterward looks at her and himself in amazement and chagrin, the novelist is depicting an important relationship between mind and body.

In middle life the sexual involution begins. At the end the difference between the old man and the old woman is largely a matter of personality and of the general habits of life. Sexual differentiation has regressed into the colorlessness of senility, and bisexuality is becoming nonsexuality.

All these cases illustrate somatopsychics, the dependence of mind on body. We do not need to visit a hospital to find many small but revealing examples of the same principle. When a man suffers the pain, let us say, of a toothache, he may shift very radically from being an active and able extrovert to being a miserable introvert whose chief concern is a relatively unimportant disability. Or when a man is very tired, he may lose his ambition, his drives, his courage to face the future, and even his most sustaining ideals. With rest and sleep, the recuperation process, he is himself again.

Language and custom recognize this dependence of mind upon body by the greetings with which men meet and conciliate one another. "How do you do? How do you feel? How are you?" are inquiries which state unequivocally that the bodily condition is the most important matter in the scheme of life.

One of my father's stories was a crude but realistic statement of the low origin of mood and purpose. Voltaire and an Englishman, so goes the tale, discussed the worth of living and decided that the ills of life outweighed its benefits. Agreeing that it was logical and wise to commit suicide, they appointed a time and place to do so. On the day set aside for this unpleasant assignment, only the Englishman appeared at the rendezvous. He looked high and low and finally discovered the philosopher in his own home, seated before a well-laden breakfast table, reading a salacious novel, and apparently well pleased with himself and the world. "This," said the Englishman, "was the day on which we were to commit suicide." "Ah," said the sage, "we agreed on that the day before yesterday; today my bowels moved."

"As is digestion, so is mind," is an old folk observation which has no complete statistical correlation, but nevertheless expresses a fact. Every fever that produces a delirium, every blow on the head that changes personality, every drug that alters consciousness, solidly establishes the thesis of the dependence of mind upon body. Every time a brain tumor is successfully removed and an altered personality thus restored, there is an example of what I have called somatopsychics.

I am firmly convinced that mood and intensity of desire are largely dependent on *coenesthesia* — that is, the sensory flow of impulses from the gut, kidney, lungs, and other internal organs back to the brain. Awareness of these impulses is usually only in the background of consciousness, but is intimately linked up with the state of well-being. To the individual his own inner state is of more intimate and intricate importance than is the rest of the universe. While James and Lange were undoubtedly wrong when they stated that people were sad because they cried and happy because they laughed, the overstatement has been beneficial because it brought mind and body into a unity unusual for philosophers.

Just as the organic condition of the body influences the emotions, so are all the emotions great organic events, reverberating in their effects and consequences throughout the body. If I should be menaced by a wild animal, my immediate reaction would be one of fear. I would express this fear by certain outward physical responses, such as a pallor of the skin, a dilatation of the pupils, a drying up of saliva, perhaps a shaking of the muscles of the body, and a marked increase in pulse rate with or without a rise in blood pressure. There would also be a shift of blood supply from the inner structures like the gastrointestinal tract to the muscles of outward movement and activity, with an associated shift of sugar from liver to muscles, the better to supply them with combustible material. Probably the chemistry of every structure in my organism would change. When a man faces a wild animal, these reactions are relevant and even necessary. If his physical response is not too great, it will be useful in giving him an increased capacity for flight. If it is excessive and causes him to faint, then, of course, it will be useful only to the threatening beast.

When we consider less dramatic situations, we find that in many individuals excessive and continued fear creates such pathology as duodenal and gastric ulcers, responses that do not assist the individual to meet the situation and are not relevant. But the normal organic reverberation to anger, fear, disgust, curiosity, or sorrow is relevant to the situation and produces appropriate responses.

Disgust most obviously creates physical response. One shows disgust either by spitting, by ejecting the offensive object from the mouth before it reaches the inner sanctum of the gastrointestinal tract, or else by symbolic or actual retching, nausea, and vomiting. "It makes me sick" is a true analysis of disgust from the visceral standpoint. Disgust can destroy sleep, reverse the action of the gastrointestinal tract, alter the energy output of the individual, just as it may in small doses increase the energy with which he attacks the problems of crudity and ugliness. A situation evoking chronic disgust lowers energy, mood, appetite for enjoyment of life in every direction. More chronic than fear, it impresses itself even more deeply on the conduct of the individual. It usually takes on the aspects of hatred. It can become the origin of a grim will to destroy. It corrodes relationships and accounts for more emotional separation of marriage-mates than does any other single affect.

We can extend this discussion *ad infinitum*. Anger tenses the body for conflict; joy capers; sorrow brings about flexor attitudes of retreat and slows down activity. Passion may be brought about by a trifle and destroyed by a minor disharmony. A look or a word may produce virility and readiness, and a look or a word may destroy both. Curiosity, wonder, awe — all these emotional states are as organic as life itself.

The effect of the emotions in disturbing bodily functions has led to a new name for an old scientific approach. The finest collection of psychosomatics can be found in *The Anatomy of Melancholy*, which Robert Burton wrote in the seventeenth century. He points out by countless citations (which violate every law of proof) that melancholy (or adverse emotion) may cause everything from heart disease to ingrowing toenails. The new *psychosomatics* emphasizes bodily changes due to psychoanalytic stresses, and attributes heart disease, accidents, and skin eruptions to foiled aggression or other complexes.

Psychosomatics is valid in so far as it states that mind and body are one; that what we call states of mind always are translated into bodily events; and that emotion, mood, and even thought become organic. But to select, as some psychosomaticists do, a single psychological event or psychological trend means that one has excluded all other possibilities or, more cogently, all interactions, including those of heredity, physical structure, diverse and conflicting personality trends, as well as chance itself.

Psychosomatics is guilty of the *selective fallacy*. Suppose a man breaks his leg *because* he stumbles over a stick, *because* he is old and feeble and cannot right himself, *because* he has imperfect co-ordination, *because* he is in a panic to catch his train, *because* he is so nearsighted that he cannot see the stick, or *because* a mischievous boy camouflaged the stick so it could not be seen. A psychoanalyst writing a book on psychosomatics might find an explanation for that broken leg in a dominating mother who aroused such violent hatred in her son that years later he punished himself by breaking his leg. By neglecting all other possible factors, the psychosomaticist proves his point and gets a tidy psychological explanation. The only disadvantage of all this is that it appeals to the uncritical and is entirely worthless as judged by the principle of proof. It is another example of the slender thinking that rushes from a few facts to ultimate generalities blown up, like a balloon, nearly to the point of bursting. The actual statistics in psychosomatics are abominable and prove nothing at all.

It is probable that any long-continued adverse emotion

creates permanent bodily changes. The influence of the emotions on the circulation, and especially in increasing heart and arterial disease, is slowly approaching the position of a definitely accepted theory of medicine. The effect of the emotions on the gastrointestinal tract is seen every day, in the raising and lowering of appetite, in the creation of spastic constipation and diarrhea, in minor and major ailments of nutrition and evacuation. The urinary tract is extremely susceptible to emotion, and frequent urination is one of the commonest signs of a perturbed mind dealing, let us say, with the highest æsthetic and moral problems.

It is undoubtedly true that there are certain physical changes due to training, conditioning, and the life circumstances which may alter bodily structure in somewhat the same way although to a lesser extent than do food, oxygen, vitamins, chemicals, and minerals of all sorts. Why not?

The paradox remains: bodily states are really greatly altered by mental events, yet much of psychosomatics is nonsense. The point is that the various states of mind are themselves dependent upon bodily conditions, and bodily conditions are equally dependent upon the states of mind. The road from mind to body is never one way; it is a constantly repetitive and surging two-way street.

Chapter XV

CONCERNING INTELLIGENCE

W<small>E</small> discuss intelligence as if it were a single attribute of the human being, the one that some might say distinguishes man from the beast. But intelligence is really no unit at all. When we so consider it, we are influenced by that fallacy which underlies words, which makes us think that because a word is a unit, the things it symbolizes are unitary. Intelligence is the many capacities to remember events and to organize them into more or less permanent settings of the personality.

Intelligence is an instrument that corresponds to the general nature of the person who owns that instrument. For the run of men, intelligence is mainly used in the service of the gastrointestinal and genitourinary tracts, to acquire food and the subsistence of life, to gain and hold the object of desire, to modify the sexual conduct. Abstract thinking, the intellect, reason, so to speak, is of value to only a very few. Even these few in most of their relationships to life use their intelligence as a tool to gain benefits more mundane than the pleasures of abstract thinking.

A man may be very capable so far as the acquisitive side of intelligence is concerned; that is, he may have a great capacity for storing away experience presented to him second-hand in books and in school; yet he may be a fool, even feebleminded, in his acts, and lack the ability to control or organize his emotions and instincts. "I am impressed," my father said, "with the fact that the more learned a man is, the more ways he knows of making a fool of himself. Stupid people know only a few ways to reach disaster. The intelligent, gifted with more imagination, know many more ways to ruin." However, he corrected this pessimism very quickly: "I will take the perils of intelligence," he said, "as against the safety of stupidity."

Among the many functions of intelligence is its role in modifying, elaborating, or restraining the instinctive drives and emotions. In this capacity intelligence makes conduct flexible by linking it up with all kinds of past experience and by bringing into play the total personality of the individual. Thus when a man is roused to rage and ready to do battle, his intelligence may step into the picture and say: "Halt! This is not the time nor the place. Wait. Conduct yourself in accordance with this, that, or the other thing; in accordance with the dignity of your station or, perhaps more cogently, the safety of the situation. . . . This man is stronger than you, or he is your employer, or your superior officer; swallow down your anger and your pride." Or, in a sexual situation, instinct urges the individual on to the consummation of his desires. Intelligence again says: "No, this is not the time nor the place. Wait for a better opportunity." Or it says: "This is wrong; you must not do it. People will say what a bad man you are."

Intelligence, then, is one of the chief devices in the concealment-revealment mechanism of man. The infant who follows his natural impulses, and so reveals without artifice and conceals nothing, becomes in the course of his development an *actor* who reveals and conceals himself in greater or lesser part according to the formulæ, necessities, and artificial compulsions of the society in which he lives. Under the government of the intelligence, the personality evolves from naïve activity to purposive acting, from unsophisticated, primitively motivated conduct to histrionic, socially conditioned conduct. This involves the polarity of concealment and revelation.

The individual must conceal a great deal of what he thinks and feels, he must squelch and inhibit his instinctive or emotional conduct, because his native thoughts and feelings, drives and desires, are considered illegitimate, obscene, criminal — or perhaps only in bad taste. When a man has a tête-à-tête with a woman, it is not usually permissible for him to express many of the thoughts and feelings he may have. Words, facial expression, bodily reactions, all must act as part of the concealment mechanism. Could one, as I often tell my patients, remove the top of the most conventional individual's head and see the forbidden and obscene thoughts that constantly stream through the mind, one would be appalled at the amount that must be concealed.

Not only must the individual conceal himself successfully, but he must also reveal himself adequately and properly on the stage of life. He must show himself either in socially approved fashion or in some way to maintain or increase his status. This revelation, of course, takes on different forms with different groups of people and at different ages of life. The completely adaptable person is rough with ruffians and refined with æsthetes. Since he has both the ability to say and do the right things at the right times and the willingness to be the listener when it is another's turn for exhibition, he can be both actor and audience in appropriate fashion. This ideal is more than most of us can hope to reach, but all of us do, in some measure, use our intelligence to govern our social conduct and make it flexible.

You will remember that my father and I spoke of man as *Homo rationalis.* Another important function of the intelligence is rationalization, a process used to find a justification for conduct, to minimize one's own inconsistencies and disharmonies, to explain away greed and egoistic conduct. It has come to pass that conduct is declared to be immoral if it is too frankly egoistic, if it seeks too openly the individual advantage. So every man tends to explain his conduct on a consistent moral and ethical basis. This is the fundamental of most propaganda, and there are always voices rationalizing brutality, conquest, and the use of naked force. Preachers, statesmen, publicists of all kinds, as well as the common men of the streets, are busily engaged in rationalizing not only their own conduct but the conduct of their leaders, their countries, their churches, and their associates. When an individual declares himself to be acting in accordance with principles or ideals, when he says, for example: "I am engaged in scientific research to advance learning," not "to gain a professorship or to be esteemed by my fellows," he is probably rationalizing in large measure. The fundamental motive of most men, no matter how idealistic their work may seem or be, is self-aggrandizement. This is a perfectly natural, normal, and proper motivation, and one that will never disappear from the life of man. But just as conduct must wear the cloak of rationalization, so must motives be disguised and transformed in accordance with the ethics of the group. Depending on the intelligence of the rationalizer, rationalization may be feebleminded, mediocre, talented, or partaking of genius. The instrument of this transformation into the permissible, accepted, and proper is intelligence.

One of the chief functions of intelligence is to delay the fulfillment of desire. Man, says Professor William E. Hocking, can enlarge the vestibule of his desires to infinity. Interpreted more literally, he can await his satisfactions in a future that may never come. For the individual the price of civilization is the suppression of many of his present natural urges in order to pursue activities that society may, at some future date, reward.

As the child becomes the youth, he is taught to deny his spontaneous vagrant impulses and yield to the demands of a culture that organizes him for a restricted life. The present moment says: "Go out and play; run and romp in the grass; talk to that pretty girl; make love to her; swim in that brook; fish; lie in the sun." The future says: "You have to pass examinations. . . . You must learn to be a farmer . . . a mechanic . . . a doctor . . . a lawyer . . . a writer . . . a business man. Therefore turn away from the present with its allurements and its seduction."

Man's intelligence enables him to live in the past and projects him into the future. It leads him, too frequently.

to deny the only reality, the present moment. It is intelligence that *creates* the future, intelligence that has its anatomical seat in the forebrain, its main instrument in language, and its chief inciter in that continuity of life which has been built up by society.

The organization of activity for the future means creating a form of social ambivalence, the denial of the present moment. This, I think, is the chief strain in man's life, a strain easily endured by a fortunate few, troublesome and disturbing to many, and tragic to others. I think I can safely say that the unorganized have less mental disease and more social mishap, and the organized have more mental disturbance and less social disaster. Those who can live both in the present and in the future are gifted in their nature.

Intelligence not only creates a future of possible rewards, but also creates for the sensitive person a future in which he, as an individual, will no longer exist. Intelligence makes the reflective man aware of the certainty of his own death. For some, the pessimists, this foreknowledge makes present and future equally valueless.

"What profit hath man of all his labor wherein he laboreth under the sun?" asked an ancient Hebrew. "I looked on all the works that my hands had wrought; and, behold, all was vanity and a striving after wind. . . . For that which befalleth the sons of men befalleth beasts; even one thing befalleth them: as the one dieth, so dieth the other . . . all are of the dust, and all turn to dust again." And our common expression: "What's the use — first an egg and then a feather duster!" is a modern reaction to the same reality.

This note of pessimism has echoed throughout the ages. "Eat, drink, and be merry, for tomorrow we die," is the essence of Omar Khayyám's philosophy, and no one has more aptly stated this side of the case of Man *vs.* Death. Indeed, many a man who has never heard of Omar has recklessly plunged into dissipation on the thoroughly pessimistic theory of "a short life and a merry one."

Other men, appalled by the brief tenure of life and the haphazard way death strikes, work hard, spurred on by the wish to leave behind great works that will live on and extend the mortal span. Many a father and mother, looking at *their* children, consider them part of their compensation for mortality. "I shall die and leave someone behind me" means "I shall die and yet I shall, in another form, live." Part of the incentive to parenthood, in a time that knows how to prevent parenthood and shirks it as disagreeable, is the fear of death, of personal annihilation.

There is a still larger reaction to the fear of death. The feeling of likeness is part of the feeling of brotherhood, and in death is one of the three great likenesses of man. We are born of the labor of our mothers; our days are full of strife and trouble; and we die. The reflective minds of humanity have lingered on these facts and felt that here was the unity of man, here the basis of brotherhood. Behind every appeal for racial unity there is the note: "Do we not all die? Why, then, should we hate one another?"

There are many who would agree with the rationalist philosophers of the eighteenth century that the road to human welfare lies in the exercise of the intelligence. Professor Morris R. Cohen, in *Reason and Nature*, proclaimed reason the final instrument of government of the life and destiny of man. On the other hand, there is a very formidable philosophical and social-theological group that attacks reason and intelligence as valid directive forces. The scorn poked at the professor and the high-brow is indicative of this underlying dislike and fear of intelligence. The claim made for woman that she has an intuition superior to intelligence in discerning the real facts of existence and the real meaning of life is her attack and the attack of her proponents on intelligence. Even Ecclesiastes, that great book of wisdom, is so pessimistic about the enduring values of wisdom that the preacher finally states: "Of making many books there is no end; and much study is a weariness of the flesh."

Philosophers such as Bergson attacked the intellect on the ground that it can reveal to us only the form and the mechanism of things; that the inner aspect of reality is known only by intuition. Most people, even most of the leading spirits of our times, do not believe that reason is the road to salvation.

In *Social Evolution* Benjamin Kidd boldly claimed that the amelioration of the world is due not to intelligence but to the growth of religious feeling and its development and extension into human relationship. This writer makes a point of the greatest importance, that material intelligence builds up crowded cities and slums, produces techniques of greater power and of greater destruction, but does not in itself and of itself lessen human suffering or bring about a scheme of life to which the idealist can subscribe.

The idea of human equality, Kidd states, has come

from religion. With this ideal, tenderness has crept into
the social scheme. Tenderness as a governing force in in-
terpersonal relationships is a comparatively recent development. It did not operate in many of the earlier cultures,
such as the Greek and Roman, however intellectual and
brilliant they were. Today the child is no longer a slave
of his parents, and tender treatment of him has become
paramount in the social scheme. Tenderness and equality
have infused into the sexual relationship. The woman
is no longer the vassal of the man, but has her own personality and her own personal rights. Although there
were cultures that insisted:

A woman, a dog, and a walnut-tree,
The more you beat 'em the better they be,

wife-beating has disappeared from modern civilized communities. The sailor is no longer flogged with the cat-o'-
nine-tails. The harsh treatment of prisoners is disappear-
ing. The horrors of the insane asylum have been replaced
by at least an approximation to humanity, and the conception that has done away with the word "lunatic" has
banished brutality and harshness of treatment. So in a
thousand and one directions we can see the growth of
personal tenderness — in a word, kindness. No longer
does one see in the city streets men with slit noses and
hands chopped off, nor are scolds any longer imprisoned
in stocks or exposed to the contumely of the mob. Even
cruelty to animals is legally proscribed, as well as fiercely
resented and punished. This is a hopeful sign.

At least it would be hopeful if there were not a per-
sistence of group ferocity, group cruelty, and great group
oppression. It is a curious anomaly, and one that strikes

the heart with terror, that with the growth of individual tenderness man has developed the capacity and the will to destroy his fellow men wholesale in a way unparalleled in all of the sorry tales of man's history. In this connection Kidd cites the immortal words of Huxley, who, as he looked around the world and saw how few there were who were removed from bestial struggle for existence, how disproportionately the goods of the world were distributed, how sordid, lonely, and silently suffering most of human existence was, stated that unless some better scheme could be evolved, he would welcome the kindly comet that would sweep the whole sorry mess into nothing.

To many an observer it has seemed as if the chaos out of which the cosmos has been evoked was a transformed chaos of increased power and deliberate destructiveness, seeking its own original state of nothingness. Yet man has compensation for his tribulations in life and his foreknowledge of death: he has his belief in immortality. While most modern science is thoroughly agnostic, in recent years such eminent scientists as Jeans, Millikan, and Lodge have striven to give some validity and scientific support to belief in immortality. Their type of immortality and their mathematical god are, however, quite thin and tenuous and do not satisfy the craving for the substantial immortality by which the individual is transplanted, body and soul, into the land of his heart's desire, to be cared for by a benevolent Father.

A nonrational faith is generally more comfortable than a rational skepticism. So, opposed to intelligence, is faith or credulity, the willingness to accept authority in order to have a solid base for one's life. Religion, as the chief expression of faith, tries to explain the meaning of life and direct the technique of living. And the church has always believed that the road to salvation lies through faith, which is nonrational. Faith may even be boldly proclaimed to be nonrational, as when St. Paul defined it as the capacity to believe in the unseen and the unproved, and when Tertullian proudly said: "I believe because it is absurd," placing absurdity above intelligence as a value for the human being.

On the one hand, when we consider the age-old battles of Science and Religion, we find intelligence opposed to faith. On the other hand, we find that intelligence must support faith as a fundamental and necessary herd instinct which preserves social solidarity. The common man cannot be comforted by the facts and theories of science. And where intelligence disintegrates faith and belief, there is also the danger that it will disintegrate the nonrational basis of society, for life is fundamentally nonrational. In fact, if one depended upon the proved in life, one would have almost nothing to depend on. Life's strivings and purposes do not, on the whole, correspond to values that we can prove valid. Although scientists postulate a purpose in all living things, that purpose is survival, reproduction, continuance to living. Behind all this there may be some purpose of an infinite scope. This we can only believe through faith.

The intelligence of man has created a social structure that presses heavily upon him, inhibiting and sometimes deforming his deep biological drives. To harmonize the pressures exerted by society and by the individual's drives is the greatest single problem of human life.

I believe that there will come a time when the divergence between biological adaptation and social adjustment will receive impartial, clear-headed, modern consideration. I am not advocating any radical social therapeutics at this or any other point. I merely say that little in life is rational: the instincts and biological drives have just enough brain to guide them to their goal, and the necessary social regulations make no sense either. Perhaps we can find some wisdom to guide us, some discipline that does not crucify the powerful longings and instinctive cavortings of man and yet leads to order, decency, and kindness. We need a way of life in which the animal, guided by reason, may romp but will not bite. A society in which men can live ethically, wisely, and at the same time enjoyably is a dream of the medical idealist. This is his Utopia, his best of all Never-Never Lands.

THE GROWTH OF THE BOOK

E<small>XCERPTS FROM CORRESPONDENCE BETWEEN</small>
A<small>BRAHAM</small> M<small>YERSON AND</small> A<small>LFRED</small> A. K<small>NOPF</small>

December 10, 1930

Dear Dr. Myerson,

If you have in preparation or in mind any book intended for the general reader, I should be extremely happy to be able to consider it for publication. . . .

Looking forward to hearing from you,

Alfred A. Knopf

January 2, 1931

Dear Mr. Knopf,

Your letter of the tenth of December has remained unanswered, largely because I have been formulating in my mind a book for which I have gathered a good deal of material over many years and which, in a sense, represents my mature point of view and is a sort of opus magnum.

The book would center around what I call "the illusion of individuality" and that might well be its title, although I am not wedded in any indissoluble way to the name. The point of departure for the book would be the fact that it is a naïve point of view to regard each individual as bounded by his skin; that this represents, so to speak, his visible, palpable boundary, but is not in any logical or scientific sense his physiological or psychological limit.

In a physiological way, it can easily be shown that there stream through each individual the materials of the environment and that foodstuffs, gases, rays of light, and energy waves pass in and out of him continually; that the gases of the environment are consumed in him to produce energy, and the products pass back into the environment in a never ending stream; that calcium, phosphorus, salts of many kinds, iron, and so forth, have a cycle of distribution which includes for a short time a stay within the living body. As a man eats, he incorporates within himself Nebraska, China, India, and the thousand and one places from which the foodstuffs come, and, in a larger sense, incorporates within himself the sun, and possibly, if Millikan is right, almost infinite sources of energy.

In a psychological sense we live in a pool of thoughts, feelings, deeds, which flow in and out of us, which become incorporated into our psyche, which organize our activity and energy. There is a veritable stream of feeling from man to man, so that the "illusion of individuality" reaches its height in the belief of an individual that he is separate from the rest of mankind; that his will is his own; that his thoughts, deeds, and feelings are *sui generis*.

The elaboration of this thesis shows that with the development of speech and writing man has extended his mental environment to his remotest ancestors and to his farthest contemporaries; that in a very real sense Plato still lives, exerting an extraordinary influence on the thoughts of man; that the nomadic Jews of the days of Abraham play a role in the thinking of every man, organizing and disorganizing our contemporary life, so far as the records of these nomads exercise a harmonious or disharmonious influence on our times.

Thus, in both a physical and a mental sense, the "illusion of individuality" is a falsification of reality, although I shall by no means say that individuals do not exist and that the illusion is a bad one, but will simply emphasize how much the world is one organism.

This thesis can be applied to the question of the relative importance of heredity and environment. In several scientific publications of my own, as well as in the gradually increasing trend in biology, the point is emphasized that there is no real separation between these two sets of forces; that hereditary trends, so-called, in each individual are modified, thwarted, fostered by the environment, and that no characteristic which manifests itself is heredity alone, but that it is a resultant of the inner and outer forces. Furthermore, a very large amount of work has been done to show that the environment can be focused upon the hereditary substances to produce new forms, new hereditary line-ups, new genetic possibilities, or to destroy, modify, and thwart existing potentialities.

In other words, our conception of eugenics must take into account that no eugenics is a matter of breeding alone, but is fundamentally an evaluation of the interplay between environment and hereditary substances; that the way to a better race is not by coupling certain males and females together, or by preventing the coupling of other males and females, but that there must be added to this all-too-simple technique a betterment of environmental conditions and those fundamentals which involve the vitality and health of the germ plasm. . . .

While the feeling of individual worth and dignity is one of the aims of society and must remain so, it must be tempered by an understanding that in large measure it is an illusion; that direction of personality, growth, and the vigor of its reactions to life are in large measure environmental; that there is a real flow from each individual to every other, which must be understood to produce not only better personalities but a more prosperous and more satisfactory society.

As a busy practitioner of medicine it will be impossible for me to devote much consecutive time to this book. I will not be able to get it ready before the end of the summer.

Very sincerely yours,
A. Myerson

March 7, 1931

Dear Dr. Myerson,

On my return from abroad I saw your interesting letter. I am delighted to know that there is a chance of our having a book from you.

I hope to be in Boston within a month and I shall give myself the pleasure of calling on you.

Yours faithfully,
Alfred A. Knopf

September 16, 1937

Dear Dr. Myerson,

 I am just wondering if you haven't in mind for possible publication a book in which I would be interested. It is a long time since I heard from you and I want you to know of our continuing interest.

 With kind regards, I am

Yours sincerely,
Alfred A. Knopf

September 22, 1937

Dear Mr. Knopf,

 Your letter was rather timely inasmuch as I had just started collecting the materials for a book to which I have given no particular name except that I have thought of it in a general way as "Leaves from a Psychiatrist's Notebook." It happens that a good deal of the work represents what might be called semi-philosophic and scientific reflections carried on in the middle of the night, since I have a habit of spending an hour or two, somewhere between 1.00 and 2.00 in the morning, mentally roaming over my experiences. The book becomes a sort of series of essays based on cases which constitute a wide range of human experience and difficulty.

 There is, first of all, a general section dealing with the attempt of society to discipline the body organs of man and the conflict that has thus arisen between morals and customs on the one side and physiology on the other. . . . The native drives of man, of his endocrines and his glands, are disciplined by society, with a resultant inner conflict of a physiologic type which takes place when the drives refuse to be disciplined or do not understand the nature of the moral teaching, so to speak; when between the forebrain as the organ of social contact and the testicle, for example, there takes place a conflict which has its important bearings for the psychiatrist and for society as a whole.

The question, of course, needs to be raised whether we are yet at the stage where society can build up a morality based on physiology, although it is certain that we should take physiology into account, so that the social structure will not bear so heavily upon man. This, of course, brings up the related problems of body-hatred, asceticism, obscenity, and, naturally enough, the sexual life of man.

As important as this series of problems is that which relates to the general activity of man. Activity is organized by society. There are certain activities which become prohibited, and certain ones which become praised and extolled, each society developing its own trends in this matter. More important is the fact that as society becomes definitely built up and organized, the individual has to build up and organize his activities *so that his spontaneous, non-purposive activities have to be sacrificed.* This may be put in another way — the present moment and its pleasures and activities have to yield to the exigencies and demands of a future which may never give pleasure or satisfaction. This brings about strain and fatigue. . . .

The strains of life become exceedingly interesting to

me in my daily practice, and I have indicated them in some of my books and writings, but I have never gathered them together for a widespread discussion. Consequently, the question of rest and recuperation becomes all-important; the nature of sleep, relaxation, exercise — these form integral and interrelated parts of therapeutics, both individual and social.

I wind up with a sort of doctor's Utopia, a land where life has become organized in relationship to the natural capacity and directions of the organs of man so as to bring about health in a widespread sense. I assume that if there is any one Good upon which man agrees, it is that health is essential to efficiency, happiness, and the general fulfillment of the individual in life. Consequently, whatever social changes are made, we have first to start with the question: Is this particular change of our social structure good or bad in relationship to the health of man? Whatever social steps need to be taken must be justified first upon the basis of their bearing on the health of man. No abstract property principles and no abstract moral principles must stand in the way of the fulfillment of the attainment of the health of man.

It would take too long to develop this theme further. You can, I think, see the general trend of the book. . . . It indicates therapeutics more than it prescribes. The therapeutics of the individual life may be laid down with certain detail and with some success, but social therapeutics, which is more important, is more dubiously and less certainly prescribed.

Very sincerely yours,

A. Myerson

April 10, 1941

Dear Knopf,

Enclosed you will find the first chapter of a book which I have long contemplated, and which your recent visit has powerfully stimulated me to write. This first section is, in a sense, deeply personal, since it depicts the man who in a very large and important way is responsible for many of my traits and capacities — my father. It also contains a point of view about life and man which he and I formulated after much discussion, during the years from my puberty to the time when I was fifty-seven years old.

What I intend to do is to elaborate some of the theses contained in this first chapter and illustrate and amplify on the basis of my clinically social experience, passing into the fields of Sex, Crime, Fatigue, Maladjustment, and then, after discussing many other phases of clinical experience, to pass into the broader questions which underlie the whole riddle of existence — the nature of the relationship between the body and the mind; the capacity for social union and wise administration of power possessed by man; the relationship for that grim force called heredity; and the as grim environment which man builds up, including his institutions, his writings, and his speech — in short, his words. It will not be a hopeful, pleasant book necessarily, or even probably, though it will contain germs of hope and a sketch of embryonic possibilities for the real living for man. It will not be dispassionate and objectively scientific, since it is a personal document, and no man is objective as a person.

Read it over when you have time, and see whether it strikes a keynote that you like.

As ever, yours,
Myerson

April 14, 1941

Dear Myerson,

Go to it — the stuff is superb. It is difficult to judge from so short a sample, but all I can say is that it confirms my conviction that you owe it to yourself, to me, and to the more intelligent part of the reading public to get busy with your writing. . . . Give me more.

Yours always,
Knopf

April 16, 1941

Dear Knopf,

Your letter was most heartening and I think I have grimly set my jaws mentally and physically for the task of writing this book. To do so, I shall have to adopt a fatalistic attitude toward the world events which hover like a nightmare on every reflective mind. Perhaps that is all the more reason for getting this book out of my system.

From time to time, therefore, I shall probably send you parts of the manuscript and get your criticism and suggestions.

Cordially yours,
Myerson

June 26, 1941

Dear Knopf,

Just to show you that I am a man of my word, I shall have ready by next Thursday the first draft of about fifty thousand words of the book. . . . The way I am going now, which I may say is at high speed, I shall have the first draft of the book finished by September.

If you will be in town during July, I shall probably drop in to see you.

Yours,
Myerson

July 2, 1941

Dear Knopf,

I am sending you by accompanying mail the first few sections of the book. I take it that you have the first section, Sketch of My Father, which is the introduction. Then comes The Great Riddle, which deals with the riddles of purpose and life, as well as the nature of and controversy about consciousness. The third is a long section which deals with the point of view taken about Mind, etc., in the book. The fourth deals with the Predominance of Means over Ends, which I find to be a profoundly important factor in human life.

I intend to go on from this point to a discussion of heredity and environment; then the energies, desire, satisfaction, and the impairment of these in disease and as a result of our culture and civilization. The section on desire and satisfaction will represent one of the most cogent parts of my work, although I have not yet written much about it. I have attempted to formulate in recent years the laws of desire and satisfaction, since healthy desire and healthy satisfaction are the essentials of healthy living.

Yours,

Myerson

October 6, 1941

Dear Knopf,

This summer has been a very busy one for me and also one in which my energies were drained away from writing by various other matters, especially those connected with the development of research throughout the United States in mental disease and the participation of psychiatrists in the defense program. So I have been able to accomplish much less than I had hoped to do. However, in the interstices of my time, I have managed to do something.

I have corrected in a fairly thorough manner the first draft of the material I sent you and I have also written and corrected a very long section on Heredity and Eugenics, as well as the relationship of genius to mental disease and suchlike matters.

We are now engaged in the sections on the energies of man with especial relationship to fatigue, frustration, appetites, desire in their relationship to the social structure. This is going to be a difficult section to write, but I have been busily engaged in thinking and writing on the problem for many years, so I think I can do it all right.

There will be two more sections, according to the plan, following this. One will be on the question of a psychopathic society; that is, a society which is not adapted to the nature of man and the consequent strains, but, more importantly, the favoring of relatively psychopathic individuals and the punishment of a good many relatively normal persons. In other words, the standard of personality and character is, in large measure, false, and consequently adjustment is exceedingly difficult for people who are biologically normal.

The final chapter will probably be short and will be a cautious attempt to define a society which will be relatively normal or at least human, since normal is not a term easily applied. . . .

Cordially yours,
Myerson

November 30, 1943

Dear Myerson,

Well, papa, here's that horrid man around again. What's happening to the book? I suppose I know the answer — nothing at all — but I'm a glutton for punishment. So tell me the bad news.

Yours always,
Alfred A. Knopf

December 7, 1943

Dear Knopf,

This "papa" business would be all right if you were a dame instead of a grizzled veteran (my wife says you aren't grizzled) of many publishing campaigns. However, it may interest you to know that I now have a literary secretary and thus it is perfectly possible that I can be pushed into writing the book. My intentions are strictly honorable. I intend to write that book and, in fact, I intend to write it all over again, except for the first and introductory section.

Since you are the guy that may publish it if (my wife says "when") I write it, here's the plan: Since my father and I discuss man in his many aspects of *Homo biologiens, Homo sensualis, Homo ferociens, Homo ambivalens,* etc., etc., the chapter headings will correspond to these terms, winding up in a great flurry of trumpets and inspiring bugle calls in the chapter to be entitled "*Homo gregariens* or Psychopathic Society."

I think I will begin the book with the question: "What is man?" and end with the sentence: "This is man." Now the book is all written, you see. I have the beginning and the end. All I have to do is put some 100,-000 or so words in between.

Best wishes,
Abe Myerson

April 20, 1944

Dear Myerson,

Could you have lunch with me on Monday, May 8th? I'll be in Boston for two or three days then. It is always a pleasure to have a gossip with you, though

my belief in your book is a little more an act of faith
than it used to be. . . .

    With kindest regards,

Yours sincerely,
Alfred A. Knopf

February 5, 1945

Dear Myerson,

    I leave you alone pretty much between my
annual visits, but I hope your conscience is eating you
up anyway. . . .

Yours always,
Alfred A. Knopf

February 19, 1945

Dear Knopf,

    Thanks for your kind wishes about my con-
science, but I assure you that where it hurts me most is
that I haven't had time to do some very urgent medical
writing. I should dearly love to write that book, but as
time goes on, it seems even more remotely possible than
before. Perhaps I'll be able to take six months off some
day . . . .

As ever yours,
Myerson

January 4, 1947

Dear Alfred,

      I have a book in my system, small and pungent, which I have already started. . . . It is going to be called *In Defense of Mom*. It will deal with the contradictory barrage of opinion to which she has been subjected and will lightly and satirically point out how bewildered she must be, and how these contradictory opinions have crept into homes to make a problem of every child, especially of the children of the literate.

      Do you want it?

Cordially yours,
Abe

January 7, 1947

Dear Abe,

      That is very good news indeed! Of course we want to see *In Defense of Mom* as soon as ever you have it ready and I cannot believe that we will not want to publish it. . . .

Yours always,
Alfred A. Knopf

April 28, 1947

Dear Alfred,

      I am sorry to say that on May 20th I shall be out of town. Otherwise I should be happy to lunch with you and Rabbi Liebman, who is a very charming gentleman.

Unfortunately, my ardor for writing books lagged again, and I am still stymied with so much scientific work and my practice that I have not had much time.

With best wishes,

Abe

November 14, 1947

Dear Abe,

I am disappointed in not having had any reply to my letter of November 11th. Would it be possible for you to lunch with me on Friday the 21st?

Yours sincerely,

Alfred

November 17, 1947

Dear Alfred,

I am sorry to have delayed an answer to your letter, but the fact is that I have been quite ill and have reached the stage where I can only do a part-time job at my office, and the rest of the time I spend in and around the bed. The condition is known as heart block and reduces the efficiency of the heart to around fifty per cent or less. At any rate, I am not particularly disturbed by the illness, but it makes it impossible for me to go out on luncheon engagements or to partake in anything but a very limited type of activity.

If you can find time to come over to 33 Taylor Crossway, we should be very happy to entertain you and talk to you on any matter which is on your mind. If the

"Malachamovis," which is my way of writing the Hebrew word for Angel of Death, does not flutter his wings too soon, I will have more time for a book.

Yours sincerely,

A. M.

February 27, 1948

Dear Alfred,

I am glad to hear you are improving and that you will soon be back to your work. The best thing that ever happened to the traumatic surgeons was the introduction of skiing.

You may be interested to know that I am really working on this book with vim and vigor. The first section, or rather the first draft of the first section, will be done within a week or two. . . . This section deals with certain generalities. The second section will deal with the injuries to human desires and satisfactions.

As for my own health, it remains reasonably good so long as I strictly limit my activity. It is amazing, however, that I am getting a kick out of writing that I have not had for years; that my tongue is in my cheek a good deal of the time as I write, so that my severe illness has not brought me any nearer to sainthood or preparations for such a beatific state.

As ever,

Abe

March 18, 1948

Dear Alfred,

I am sending you what is about the first half of my book. At my rate of progress, I will probably be through with it by the end of the summer. . . .

Cordially,

Abe

August 14, 1948

Dear Alfred,

I have gone through the dark tunnel two or three times since we last corresponded, which means in plain language that on those occasions I was at death's door, and the situation demanded desperate measures, which were taken with success.

I must confess that I have been badgered and beaten in a way that has kept me from doing much work. In fact, there were whole weeks in which I was unable to lift my arms or raise my voice to the point requisite for any work. Still, I kept the idea of the book in mind, have gone back to it, and find the doing of it a great help.

It will amuse you to know that I am keeping notes on my illness because, in many respects, it presents unique phenomena or at least unique so far as the literature is concerned. . . . In general, I feel quite proud of my profession, as a result of my own experience. Perhaps it is not a sample experience in that the men looking after me are bound to me by chains of affection and respect and have put in an extraordinary amount of time and effort to keep me going. Nevertheless, I look back on the period when I studied heart disease, which was thirty-five years ago, and the progress really has been something.

Believe me, I am going to try and finish the book if my strength holds out.

As ever,
Abe

ABRAHAM MYERSON:
A BIOGRAPHICAL NOTE

Abraham Myerson's personality and his career were marked by an intense thirst for knowledge and an ardent zeal to ameliorate the ills of mankind. Brilliant, scholarly, yet a plain and practical man, he reached great eminence as a neurologist and psychiatrist. He was known to a sizable fraction of New England as the understanding doctor who helped in times of sickness and trouble, to generations of medical students and young doctors as a stimulating teacher and friend, and to his colleagues throughout the world for his research, his papers, and his books.

"With great dynamic qualities of personality, with deep erudition and learning, with brilliance, wit and articulateness, with strong emotional devotion to good causes, and with a great store of energy, he was indeed a force in the medical world — local, national and international," wrote Dr. Harry C. Solomon, Professor of Psychiatry at Harvard Medical School.

Abraham Myerson was born on November 23, 1881 in the ghetto village of Yanova, Lithuania. His father, originally educated to be a rabbi, had rebelled against the absolutes, both of the orthodox faith and of the czarist state, and had become in his philosophy a confirmed agnostic and socialist, in his profession a school teacher. It was probably a tribute to Morris Myerson's acumen and ability that the pious villagers respected him despite his iconoclasm.

Interested in spreading education, he collected a small library of books, which he lent to members of the community. His project lasted until a government inspector, finding some banned volumes on his shelf, hinted that a speedy emigration might be preferable to exile in Siberia. He crossed the border into East Prussia, then went on to the United States. A year later, in 1886, his wife and family joined him in New Britain, Connecticut.

In 1892 the family moved to Boston so that the father, who had been a peddler, could start in business as a junk dealer. Living in the waterfront district of the South End, Abraham Myerson thrived on the exciting slum environment. His life as a boy was free and happy. In later years he looked upon it with great pleasure, recalling, for instance, such Tom Sawyeresque adventures as the times when he and his brother Simon, aged respectively eleven and nine, slid down from the window at midnight to row or swim in Boston Harbor.

He took an active role in the intense gang life of the neighborhood, in the battles as well as the games. Strong, agile, and (from all reports, including his own) a first-class scrapper, he quickly showed the pugnacity that was eventually to distinguish his intellectual and professional life. A few days after the family arrived in Boston, he was introduced to the acknowledged leader of the neighborhood gang. "I'll lick him in two weeks," he told his brother that evening. According to his brother, he did.

Meanwhile, the tradition of scholarship flourished in

the family. The father, who read and studied for hours every night, discussed his interests with the children. At the dinner table the family talked about historical personages with such enthusiasm and partisanship that easy conversations frequently became heated debates. When the father's fortunes improved, the family moved to a better neighborhood, where the children had the benefit also of more intellectual companions. Eventually, of the six children in this immigrant family, there were two physicians, a dentist, and a school teacher.

Abraham Myerson was well endowed for the intellectual life. He had, for instance, the ability to read very quickly — in fact, to read a printed page in a few glances. Also, at least as a young man, he had such a remarkable memory that he could as a parlor trick have someone select any page in Shakespeare, glance over it, and then repeat it word for word. When he was older, he deplored the loss of this gift, but what he considered the bare residue of his memory was nevertheless impressive.

Always an avid reader, he was at first concerned mainly with history. While he was in high school, he developed a deep interest in biology and later felt that his trend toward a scientific career began with his knowledge of Darwin, Huxley, and Spencer.

He was graduated from English High School in 1898, and worked for several years in various occupations, eventually directing his efforts toward saving enough money to go to medical school. (At that time premedical college training was not required.) He went for a year to Physicians and Surgeons at Columbia University, but had to leave school when he ran out of money. He then worked for a year as a substitute streetcar conductor, enduring the hardships of having to be on call at the carbarn for twenty hours a day, sleeping as best he could on the benches there, and working on an open platform in all kinds of weather. After a second year at Columbia he transferred to Tufts Medical School in Boston and was graduated in 1908.

His transfer to Tufts may have had a radical effect on his career, for it was there that he was a student of the brilliant, dynamic neurologist and psychologist Dr. Morton Prince. The study of the human mind, a relatively new and exciting field, appealed to him immediately. First coming to Dr. Prince's attention for his ability in brain anatomy, he joined and later was president of a club that Dr. Prince organized for discussions on psychology. His interest and obvious talent formed the basis of a lifelong friendship with his teacher. It was a matter of some pride to Myerson that he eventually held the chair in neurology which had been Morton Prince's.

After his graduation he opened an office to practice general medicine. Fortunately for his future career, he was not overwhelmed by would-be patients and had plenty of time to spend at the Boston City Hospital as an assistant in the Department for Diseases of the Nervous System. After two and a half years there, he devoted six months to neuropathology in the laboratory of Dr. E. E. Southard and then went to St. Louis, Missouri, to be resident neurologist at the Alexian Brothers' Hospital and instructor in neuropathology at St. Louis University.

In 1912 he returned to Boston to be in the first group

of residents at Boston's new Psychopathic Hospital. Then from 1913 to 1917 he was clinical director and pathologist at the Taunton State Hospital.

During a brief vacation from his position in St. Louis, Abraham Myerson had met Dorothy Loman and, within forty-eight hours, proposed to her. They were married in 1913. It proved to be an unusually fortunate marriage. Charming, capable, sympathetic, and intelligent, she shared his interests and reciprocated fully his great devotion to her.

They had three children, Paul Graves (1914), David John (1919), and Anne (1925). As a father, Myerson was most certainly stimulating, and also very kind and understanding. According to one of his friends, he had the reputation for practically doting on his children. It is undoubtedly some measure of his stature as a parent, as well as of his own contagious enthusiasm, that the two sons are now practicing psychiatrists, the daughter a psychiatric social worker.

By 1917, thanks to a tremendous output of writing and research, his reputation had spread sufficiently so that he felt ready to return to Boston and begin the private practice of neurology and psychiatry. He was immediately successful, and from then on the pattern of his professional life was clear: it consisted in research, voluminous writing, a large private practice, and teaching.

Abraham Myerson was a very attractive man, with cleanly modeled features and piercing blue eyes deeply set under heavy brows and a high forehead. Prematurely bald, except for a gray fringe, he appeared dignified, even, at times, awe-inspiring. Broad-shouldered and deep-chested, although not a heavy man, he gave the impression of strength and solidity.

Imbued with a zeal for living and a desire for experience, he found all the phenomena of life, esoteric, commonplace, queer, or conventional, grist to his mill. He was eager to know people, he was an excellent companion, and he had a great capacity for friendship. As a fascinated observer of the human scene and an omnivorous reader of philosophy, fiction, history, biography, and science, he had a range of interests which omitted very little. He had tremendous enthusiasms — over books, people, some new piece of research — and the ability to communicate his enthusiasm to others.

In his younger years he was a fervent and capable athlete, and he had throughout his life an intense admiration for the strong and well-trained body. In their boyhood he and his brother trained so assiduously in acrobatics and were so proficient that they considered making a career of the flying rings and bars. Even in his fifties Myerson could still astonish the children in the family by doing stunts they would not attempt. He enjoyed his strength and actually got pleasure from certain physical challenges. To swim in a heavy surf, to push his automobile out of a mud-hole, to jump out of bed into an icy room, or row with a summer sun shining full in his face was to him the chance to pit his strength and endurance against Nature.

Poised, forceful, sometimes practically indomitable, he was skilled in argument; he glorified in it and welcomed controversy over intellectual or scientific questions as other men welcome the competition of bridge table or golf links. Rarely willing to let a questionable statement pass unquestioned, he made the people around him learn to avoid rash generalizations. He was a very genial companion with people whom he enjoyed, but he could be abrupt and crushing to the layman who chose to instruct him in psychiatry or to anyone who propounded a mystical dogma or spoke authoritatively without the requisite knowledge.

He was always willing to fight for the right as he saw it — whether it was in his own field or in some wider social sphere — and devoted himself to social improvement and civic affairs. Since, as a student of heredity, he took the view that heredity and environment are not separable but are constantly interacting forces, his zeal for practical social improvement harmonized with his theories. It also, in a simpler way, was merely the expression of a warm and generous man.

He often quoted William James's statement that some people are born with a bottle of champagne to their credit. His own account seemingly included at least half a case. His mood was high, and although he was, intellectually, a pessimist, aware of the suffering, the disease, and the conflict in the world, he always remained, emotionally, an optimist, somehow convinced that some day there would be solutions to many of our present problems.

His energy and vigor were practically legendary. Merely to have accompanied and watched him on one of his typical working days would in itself have constituted a feat of endurance. His work day frequently stretched from half past six in the morning until late at night. He spent an hour before breakfast going over papers or articles in preparation. By shortly after eight he was on the way from his home in Brookline to the Boston State Hospital in Mattapan. There he worked in his laboratory, going over whatever research projects were in progress, and possibly visited several other buildings of the hospital to see patients in whom he was interested. En route back to Boston, he might make a house call or visit one of the many hospitals where he was a consultant in neurology or psychiatry, and then proceed to court to testify as the psychiatric expert in either a criminal or a compensation case. Next he went to his office, where he saw a few patients before lunch. On other days he spent the late morning hours making rounds at the Boston City Hospital, where he was the chief of the neurology service.

After lunch, during the period when he was teaching, there were lectures to the Tufts medical students. Then back he went to an office jammed with his patients and their accompanying relatives and friends. (In his thirty years of private practice, and exclusive of his medicolegal work, Myerson saw somewhat more than twenty-five thousand patients.) Leaving his office at five thirty, he made a house call or two on the way home.

In the evening, if he wasn't addressing a lay group or going to a medical meeting — in other words, if it was to be merely a quiet evening at home — there was always some work to be done on a paper or book, or on one of the outspoken book reviews for which he was famous. In the final two years of his life, when he knew he must conserve his strength, he compromised with his physicians by not going to work until ten o'clock and returning home promptly by six!

Never with quite enough time to do all that he had to do, he hurried through life, briefcase in hand, and coat-tails flying behind him. Always concentrating on the lecture he was about to give, some problem in research, or something he was writing (and "Concentration," he said, "is fundamentally the capacity to exclude the non-relevant thought processes"), he was as likely as not to brush past one of his best friends without even seeing him. Because he had the capacity for excluding such thoughts nonrelevant to his work as those dealing with the whereabouts of his hat, briefcase, or key-ring, everyone who worked with him expected the daily search for at least one of these articles. And it was not unusual for a taxi-driver to appear at the Myerson home in the middle of a morning to ask for a jacket or even a tie for the doctor. On one memorable occasion he discovered on his way into the City Hospital auditorium that he was wearing neither collar nor tie. Dashing out of the hall, he jumped into his car, found a near-by haberdashery, and reappeared for his lecture only a few minutes late and quite satisfied that his students would not now be able to tag him as their absent-minded professor.

A year after Myerson returned to Boston, he became an assistant professor of neurology at Tufts Medical School. Three years later, in 1921, he was appointed professor, and held the chair until his retirement in 1940, when he became professor emeritus. He had a particular fondness for teaching and a warm regard for his stu-

dents. Thanks to his knack of finding the right analogy
or parable to explain his points, he had the ability to present difficult scientific ideas or cut-and-dried anatomical
and physiological facts in a vivid and stimulating manner.
Engaging both the interest and the affection of his students, he was one of the most popular teachers at the
school. The unusual number of Tufts students who themselves have become specialists in neurology and psychiatry has been cited by Dr. A. Warren Stearns, the former
dean of Tufts Medical School, as evidence of the way
Myerson inspired his students and transmitted to them
his own enthusiasm.

His gift for the dramatic, his wit, and his ability to
simplify complicated ideas were equally serviceable in
making him a most popular lecturer to lay groups and
writer for what he called "the intelligent, non-professional
reader."

In 1918 he wrote a few articles on the neurosis of the
housewife. These articles, appearing at a time when the
public had not yet recognized the peculiar emotional and
environmental difficulties of woman, and when "Mom"
was still a title of respect and affection, aroused a great
deal of interest and came to the attention of a publisher
who asked him to elaborate his ideas into a book. *The
Nervous Housewife*, published in 1920, was and still is
a lucid statement of the problems of the woman in our
culture. For the good reason that this book could easily
be presented by either spouse to the other, it had probably
the widest circulation of any of his popular writings.

To combat widespread ignorance about one of the
major problems of society, he wrote, in 1927, *The Psy-*

chology of Mental Disorders. "Even amongst men and women who are cultured, who can speak with some degree of assurance about vitamins, tuberculosis, and who are not afraid to venture into a discussion of the infectious diseases," he wrote, "there is only the vaguest knowledge of what constitutes mental disease." In his book he dedescribed the symptoms of the mental diseases and the neuroses and discussed the importance of the problems raised by these conditions.

If there was one characteristic that unified Myerson's career and underlay his many interests, it was his devotion to Science, to the scientific spirit of inquiry and the scientific evaluation of results. Compared with the other branches of medicine, psychiatry is inexact and still largely a realm of theory, rather than of known, provable fact. It was Myerson's ambition to enlarge the boundaries of the exact knowledge.

The first problem he tackled, that of the inheritance of mental disease, proved to be a lifelong interest. He achieved such distinction in this field that Dr. Franz Kallmann, the famous psychiatrist and geneticist, describes him as "one of the finest and most resourceful pioneer workers of psychiatric genetics."

In St. Louis, working under Dr. William Washington Graves, an outstanding neurologist with a great interest in heredity, his interest had turned to the study of families and the question of the transmission of mental disease, epilepsy, and feeblemindedness.

He returned to Boston determined to investigate the hereditary aspects of these illnesses, and when he was at Taunton found the opportunity for a thorough study. Of all the patients who had been in the hospital since it was founded in 1854, roughly ten per cent had one or more relatives who had also been hospitalized at Taunton. His study of these related patients and as many of their non-hospitalized relatives and descendants as could be interviewed or described has been called "a prodigious piece of work which gave him a leading place as an authority on the inheritance of mental disease."

This study was as accurate as he could make it, but by no means so accurate as he would have wished. To have to accept the possibly incorrect diagnoses of half a century before and rely on family hearsay for information about non-hospitalized relatives was, to Myerson, very unsatisfying. Because he felt that it was very important to know in how far the descendants of the insane contribute to society's problems — insanity, criminality, feeblemindedness, pauperism, disease — he conceived a plan of a small, permanent research organization to study the descendants of the contemporary insane over several future generations. Unfortunately there were no funds available to endow such a project.

In 1924, in *The Inheritance of Mental Diseases*, he summarized the existing theories and knowledge and set forth his own point of view. He discussed the question of whether "the transmissible mental diseases are really hereditary characters, in the sense that stature and blue eyes are hereditary characters, or whether they merely represent diseases, caused by unknown agents whose effects persist over two or more generations and from which a stock may either die or recover." While he inclined to the latter view, he felt that there would have to be much more definite information on the subject before anyone could speak authoritatively on the inheritance of mental diseases.

At about this time he headed a group to study the families of 845 inmates of two Massachusetts schools for the feebleminded. The findings, published in 1930, were, first, that feeblemindedness was not linked hereditarily with the other mental diseases, and, second, that while it did to some extent occur in close family groups, there were, in Massachusetts at least, no families corresponding in general unfitness to the classic examples, the Jukes and Kallikaks. "What we call heredity does play an important role in feeblemindedness," wrote Myerson, "but by no means the role usually ascribed to it. Much of feeblemindedness is environmental in origin, much is hereditary, but the most is of unknown origin, and may represent the inexplainable downward movement of intelligence, just as genius represents its inexplainable upward movement."

Going to the upper end of the social scale for the last of his family studies, he investigated and described the incidence of the manic-depressive psychosis in some of the most distinguished New England families, families "conspicuous for their accumulation of wealth and production of important men — chief justices, governors, men of great renown in poetry, philosophy, psychology, and science."

Myerson believed in a limited program of eugenical sterilization. He did not, however, view sterilization as a panacea and took violent exception to the extravagant measures proposed by the ardent eugenists. "Anyone who wishes for rational eugenic measures to become operative," he wrote, "must fight irrational measures, since it frequently happens that the overenthusiastic proponents of a cause hurt it more than do its enemies, as is well epitomized in the popular proverb: 'God save me from my friends; I can look after my enemies myself.' " In 1935, as chairman of a committee of the American Neurological Association, he amassed all the existing information on sterilization statutes and their enforcement in the United States and abroad, and wrote the committee report, *Eugenical Sterilization — a Reorientation of the Problem.*

Interestingly enough, because the fields would seem quite different, Dr. Myerson was as noted for his physiological research as he was for his family studies. He had two characteristics essential for success in the laboratory: an imagination teeming with ideas for new projects and experiments and the techniques for carrying them out, and a passion for exact knowledge.

In 1927 he became director of research at the Boston State Hospital. Here he accomplished what he himself considered his most important contribution to science: he perfected a safe and practical technique for obtaining blood from the internal jugular vein and the internal carotid artery. "It seemed theoretically correct," he wrote, "that if one could study the blood directly before it reached the brain, and then could study it directly as it came from the brain . . . something might be learned of what takes place within the brain." His simple technique with a needle and syringe broadened out into a new method of studying, first, the metabolism of the brain, and later, used in conjunction with spinal puncture, the interrelationships between venous pressure and spinal-fluid pressure.

His laboratory at the Boston State Hospital originally consisted of a few small basement rooms, his staff of a few physicians and one technician. In 1933 the Commonwealth of Massachusetts completed the laboratory which he had long needed and which was his dream materialized: an impressive modern three-story building, to be staffed by several physicians and three or four technicians. A grant from the Rockefeller Foundation supplied the funds for many of his projects.

In 1935, in recognition of his accomplishments in research, Myerson was appointed Clinical Professor of Psychiatry at Harvard University. In the period following he did a great deal of research on the sympathetic and parasympathetic drugs and their effects on such body functions as heartbeat, blood pressure, and the output of gastric juice.

He was intensely interested in the effect of various drugs on mood, and experimented with countless drugs, singly and in combination, in an effort to find something beneficial for depression or anxiety but without any harmful effects. He did, for instance, much of the early work on benzedrine sulphate.

In groups devoted to research Myerson held many important positions. He was, for example, for eight years the chairman of the committee on research of the American Psychiatric Association, and during the war the

American Psychiatric Association representative to the National Research Council and a member of the Advisory Council on Research in Nervous and Mental Diseases of the U.S. Public Health Service.

His interest in physiological research was based on his deep conviction of the interdependence of mind and body. From the very first his approach to psychiatry was organic, physiological rather than psychological. He felt that the great advances in psychiatry would be made through physiological treatment, be it drugs, shock, or surgery.

He welcomed every new advance in the treatment of mental disease through physical procedures, and was, of course, very enthusiastic about the technique of shock therapy, which had been developed in Europe and then introduced into the United States. Observing that it was almost miraculous to be able to interrupt a depression that, without treatment, might have lasted for months or even years, he was in the vanguard of those in this country who tried the new treatment and found it satisfactory. He then displayed his usual crusading zeal by traveling through New England to teach the technique and explain in what cases it should be used.

"The physiological approach to the neuroses does not exclude nor minimize the importance of a complete understanding of the psychological life of the individual," he said. While he conceded that the psychological approach was "valid enough from a theoretical and practical point of view," he criticized it for not being scientific. "The lack of control studies and the impossibility of introduc-

ing measurement prevent its being considered as con-
forming to the scientific method."

"Scientific psychiatry," Myerson said, "should be
skeptical, humble, and experimental." In his opinion,
neither the psychological approach in general nor the
Freudian approach in particular fulfilled this definition.

He was, in fact, for many years one of the most promi-
nent and articulate of the American opponents to psychoanalysis. Although he appreciated the greatness of
Freud and the importance of Freud's contributions to
thought, he objected to many of the specific principles of
analysis and felt an obligation to serve as a balance wheel,
to stand against what he considered unwarranted claims
made for analysis by some psychoanalysts. Once, on
hearing an analyst claim fine results in curing depression
by a combination of shock treatment and intensive psy-
chotherapy, Myerson said it reminded him of the fly,
puffing, panting, and completely exhausted "because he
and the bull had plowed the field together."

At any rate, many a medical meeting was considerably
enlivened by Myerson's attacks on the Freudians. His
pugnacity was probably best exemplified in this area of
his activity. A skilled debater, he was capable of provok-
ing his opponents into exaggerations easy to demolish or
reducing them to simmering rage. At some times he engaged in full-scale serious debate, at others contented
himself with a witty parable or devastating quip. When
a psychoanalyst attributed epilepsy to hatred for the
father, Myerson said that he had seen many epileptic
cats, none of them even knowing his father.

While he was probably intensely disliked by many

psychoanalysts, he numbered others among his close friends and with them could discuss analysis in an atmosphere of peace and amiability. It is even more notable that he did not try to discourage his older son, who was already practicing psychiatry in his office, from taking the analytic training.

In his later years his opinions were modified to the extent that he even, on a few occasions, advised patients to be psychoanalyzed. By his own admission, he lacked the patience necessary for the long and intensive treatment essential in certain types of neuroses. As for the major disorders, while he still felt certain that the future of psychiatry lay in physical therapeutics, he conceded that after drugs, shock, or surgery had been used to interrupt a mental disturbance, psychotherapeutics might prove a useful adjunct in the treatment of the patient. Above all, however, he had faith that some day the organic causes or reasons for predisposition to mental disease would be found and also that the future held better organic treatment, perhaps even cure, for these states.

As a practicing psychiatrist who had to treat his patients within the limitations of existing knowledge, he had a very keen appreciation of the psychological factors that led people to seek his help. He was known to other doctors as a brilliant diagnostician, to his patients as a warm, understanding human being from whom they could get support, encouragement, and very good advice.

In discussing his relationships with his patients, he once wrote: "I let the barriers break themselves down and help by showing that I have no moral prejudices and that as a psychiatrist I do not sit in judgment, whatever I may do as an ordinary man. One can reach professionally that pinnacle of utter objectivity where nothing is perversion, nothing sinful, nothing obscene, nothing vulgar, nothing wrong, however it may be in the living of life within a mores and a code. Whatever the deed, thought, or word may be, it is merely human conduct, wise or unwise, healthy or unhealthy, important or irrelevant."

In his treatment he disdained any system, relying, he said, on "common sense, psychological insight, and good medical judgment."

As a practicing psychiatrist he also was constantly aware of the pressure of society on the individual. "Apart from his group," Myerson said, "a man is a mere potentiality. He is developed in a milieu that fosters, modifies, or destroys his capacities. . . . To explain the individual and discuss his psychology as something distinct from the psychology of the society . . . is, as the anatomists would say, a false dissection, by which structures are isolated from one another artificially and their organic connection destroyed."

This attitude, implicit in almost all his writings, was particularly emphasized in *Social Psychology*, published in 1934. Here he discussed the social forces that take command of the individual and create "within him both the pleasures of conformity and the bitter self-dividing struggle that results from the disharmony of individual capacity and desire with social authority."

The practical applications of this attitude permeated

Myerson's views on criminality and alcoholism, two problems which are sometimes attributed to individual psychopathology, but which Myerson ascribed to wider social conditions. Over a period of eight years, as an examiner for the Commonwealth of Massachusetts, he examined more than a thousand prisoners, ranging from alcoholics to murderers, who were confined in the Dedham jail. In general, Myerson felt that crime was a matter of social definition: what is a crime in one society can be quite legal in another. More specifically, he said that probably nowhere in the modern history of science have there been more rash generalizations and more facile conclusions than in the supposedly scientific studies that find the cause of crime in the mental state of the criminal.

"By far the majority of the men I have examined in jails and prisons have not in any way impressed me as being mentally sick or psychopathic, as the term is used elsewhere in psychiatry. Nor have they shown true personality disease other than that of the common low-grade, unorganized individual, who is planless, impulsive, reckless, lacking in integration. This does not imply that they are unorganizable, or that their difficulty could not be remedied by social attention and by better training and environment; nor does it yet place the blame on the environment, for other individuals of the same family or the same social group become well-organized. It implies rather that ordinary social training and teaching is not individual enough to meet the needs of these special persons."

Myerson was known to the public as the psychiatric expert who played a role in some of the most widely fol-

lowed trials held in New England, the most famous being the trial of Sacco and Vanzetti. During his visits to
the Dedham jail he had many interviews with Sacco,
who was confined there from 1920 to 1927. He also
examined Vanzetti, who was imprisoned elsewhere, on
a few occasions. He inclined toward the opinion that
these men were innocent and felt, at any rate, that their
trial was grossly unfair.

As for alcoholism, the second problem that Myerson
attributed more to social causes than to individual psychopathology, he felt that relief of the problem would
have to come through education and social legislation.
He felt that the education should be moderate ("not the
foolishness that talks about the extremes of injury") and
that it should be implemented by taking the sale of alcohol away from the private companies who encourage its
use and putting it in the hands of a governmental agency.
To those who doubted whether such a program could be
carried out, he cited the success of a similar plan in the
Scandinavian countries. As a member of the scientific
committee of the Research Council on Problems of Alcohol, he had the opportunity to study the problems of
alcoholism and express his views.

In December 1930 Alfred A. Knopf had written to
Myerson that he would be happy to consider for publication a book intended for the general reader. Myerson
replied with great enthusiasm that for many years he had
been gathering material and formulating ideas for such a
book, which was to represent his "mature point of view
and [be] a sort of opus magnum." The two men corre-

sponded about the proposed volume until, eighteen years later, Myerson died — his book not yet published or even completed.[1]

Unfortunately for the progress of an opus magnum, Myerson could hardly find time enough for all his other activities. At several periods he managed to begin the work, to construct a general outline and even write a few chapters before his enthusiasm wilted under the pressure of duties that could not be postponed. Then, usually, years passed until an inquiry from Mr. Knopf set him to work again. Each time he returned to the writing, he had completely new plans for the organization and presentation of his ideas and chose to begin at the beginning once more. Eventually almost all of this labor was utilized: each draft of the book is to some extent apparent in the final draft. At any rate, because the book evolved so slowly and recorded his chief interests and most important observations over a period of many years, it became his opus magnum more truly than he could have foreseen.

Only during the last year of his life, when he was suffering so acutely from a cardiac condition that he had to live as a semi-invalid, could he find the leisure to work on this book. Eager to write and full of new ideas, he was anxious to complete the manuscript. Because he knew that his days were numbered, he felt that he should be working faster than ever. Yet, ironically enough, when he had finally found the time, his strength permitted only very brief periods of writing or dictation. For a man who had enjoyed a superabundance of en-

---

[1] Excerpts from their correspondence are given on pp. 234 ff.

ergy, his weakness was perhaps the hardest blow, even
harder to bear than the pain or the knowledge of approaching death.

Between his attacks he carried on as best he could,
writing and occasionally seeing patients. Then, on September 3, 1948, he died.

The manuscript he left consisted, in the first place, of
the chapters that he had most recently completed, chapters i–iv of this book and the chapter on Desire, which
was the last thing he wrote and was, evidently, to serve
as the introduction to the second section of the work.
There was, besides, a great deal of other material, which
had been written at different times, some of it in the form
of completed chapters, some in drafts that he had dictated
but never revised. There were also several short sections
on various themes.

It was my interesting task to piece this material together, attempting to make it as nearly as possible a book
he might have completed. Edith Small Myerson, offering
invaluable advice and assistance, shared the work and the
pleasure of preparing our father-in-law's manuscript for
publication. To Mollie L. Schoenberg and Miriam Gar-
field I wish to express our gratitude for their loving labors,
as well as to the other friends who were so helpful.

As a battle-scarred lecturer, Myerson was fairly re-
signed to lengthy introductions. There is a story, probably apocryphal, that at one meeting, however, all previous records were exceeded. The gentleman who was to
introduce Myerson began at eight o'clock, took many
devious detours, outlining his own ideas on philosophy,

politics, and psychiatry, and finally concluded with a flourish and the name of the speaker at quarter to ten.

"Ladies and gentlemen," Myerson began, "the human anatomy was not designed to allow for sitting quietly in one place for more than two hours. Since you have already heard a very interesting speech, I now wish you all good night."

MILDRED ANN MYERSON

BIBLIOGRAPHY OF THE WORKS
OF ABRAHAM MYERSON

BOOKS

The Nervous Housewife. Boston: Little Brown & Co.;
1920. 273 pp.

The Inheritance of Mental Diseases. Baltimore: Williams & Wilkins Co.; 1925. 336 pp.

When Life Loses Its Zest. Boston: Little, Brown & Co.;
1925. 218 pp.

The Psychology of Mental Disorders. New York: The
Macmillan Co.; 1927. 135 pp.

The Foundations of Personality. Boston: Little, Brown
& Co.; 1931. 406 pp.

The German Jew — His Share in Modern Culture. New
York: Alfred A. Knopf; 1933. 161 pp. (With
Isaac Goldberg.)

Social Psychology. New York: Prentice-Hall Co.; 1934.
640 pp.

Eugenical Sterilization — A Reorientation of the Problem. By the Committee of the American Neurological Association for the Investigation of Sterilization,
Abraham Myerson, Chairman. New York: The
Macmillan Co.; 1936. 211 pp.

SCIENTIFIC ARTICLES

(A few titles selected to show the scope of the author's
research interests)

"Psychiatric Family Studies." *Am. J. Insanity,* lxxii, 3:
355-486 (January 1917).

"Anhedonia." *Am. J. Psychiat.*, 2, 1:87-103 (July 1922).

"Technic for Obtaining Blood from the Internal Jugular Vein and Internal Carotid Artery." *Arch. Neurol. & Psychiat.*, *17*:807-8 (June 1927). (With R. D. Halloran and H. L. Hirsch.)

"Researches in Feeblemindedness with Special Relationship to Inheritance." *Bull. Mass. Dept. Ment. Dis.*, *14*:108-229 (April 1930).

"Studies of Biochemistry of Brain Blood by Internal Jugular Puncture." *Am. J. Psychiat.*, *10*:389-406 (November 1930).

"Physiological Approach to the Psychoneuroses." *Bull. Mass. Dept. Ment. Dis.*, *15*:1-9 (April 1931).

"Insulin Hypoglycemia; Mechanism of the Neurologic Symptoms." *Arch. Neurol. & Psychiat.*, *33*:1-18 (January 1935). (With W. Dameshek.)

"Neuroses and Neuropsychoses. The Relationship of Symptom Groups." *Am. J. Psychiat.*, *93*, 2:263-301 (September 1936).

"Human Autonomic Pharmacology. XII. Theories and Results of Autonomic Drug Administration." *J.A.M.A.*, *110*, 2:101-3 (January 8, 1938).

"The Legal Phases of Psychiatry." *Am. J. Med. Jurisprudence*, *1*, 2:73-8 (October 1938).

"Theory and Principles of the 'Total Push' Method in the Treatment of Chronic Schizophrenia." *Am. J. Psychiat.*, *95*, 5:1197-1204 (March 1939).

"The Attitude of Neurologists, Psychiatrists, and Psychologists towards Psychoanalysis." *Am. J. Psychiat.*, *96*, 3:623-41 (November 1939).

"The Social Psychology of Alcoholism." *Dis. Nerv. System*, *1*, 2:1–8 (February 1940).

"The Rationale of Amphetamine (Benzedrine) Sulphate Therapy." *Am. J. Med. Sci.*, *199*, 5:729–37 (May 1940).

"Experience with Electric Shock Therapy in Mental Disease." *New England J. Med.*, *224*, 26:1081–5 (June 26, 1941). (With Louis Feldman and Isadore Green.)

"The Incidence of Manic-depressive Psychosis in Certain Socially Important Families. Preliminary Report." *Am. J. Psychiat.*, *98*, 1:11–21 (July 1941). (With Rosalie D. Boyle.)

"The Sale of Alcoholic Beverages. A Proposal for Changes in the Present Methods to Conform with the Federal Food, Drug and Cosmetic Act and to Promote Public Health." *Mental Hygiene*, *26*, 2:235–42 (April 1942). (With Leo Alexander and Merrill Moore.)

"The Bisexuality of Man." *J. Mt. Sinai Hosp.*, *9*, 4:668–78 (November-December 1942). (With Rudolph Neustadt.)

"The Sleeping and Waking Mechanisms. A Theory of the Depressions and Their Treatment." *J. Nerv. & Ment. Dis.*, *105*:598–606 (June 1947).

"Scrutiny, Social Anxiety, and Inner Turmoil in Relationship to Schizophrenia." *Am. J. Psychiat.*, *105*, 6:401–9 (December 1948).

PUBLISHER'S NOTE

This book is set in an experimental Linotype face to be called STUYVESANT. *The roman characters are based on a type face cut by Jacques François Rosart (1714–77) at Haarlem about the year 1750. The roman is darker in tone than the Rosart but holds to many of the Dutch peculiarities of Rosart's letter forms. The italic of Stuyvesant is a new design, drawn in harmony with the Rosart feeling. In Stuyvesant,* W. A. DWIGGINS *has tried to preserve something of the hand-cut qualities of the earlier Dutch face — to get away, one might say, from the too great precision of the machine.*

The book was composed, printed, and bound by The Plimpton Press, Norwood, Massachusetts. The typography and binding are by Mr. Dwiggins.